The media's watching Vault!
Here's a sampling of our coverage.

"For those hoping to climb the ladder of success, [Vault's] insights are priceless."
– *Money magazine*

"The best place on the web to prepare for a job search."
– *Fortune*

"[Vault guides] make for excellent starting points for job hunters and should be purchased by academic libraries for their career sections [and] university career centers."
– *Library Journal*

"The granddaddy of worker sites."
– *U.S. News and World Report*

"A killer app."
– *The New York Times*

One of Forbes' 33 "Favorite Sites"
– *Forbes*

"To get the unvarnished scoop, check out Vault."
– *Smart Money Magazine*

"Vault has a wealth of information about major employers and job-searching strategies as well as comments from workers about their experiences at specific companies."
– *The Washington Post*

"A key reference for those who want to know what it takes to get hired by a law firm and what to expect once they get there."
– *New York Law Journal*

"Vault [provides] the skinny on working conditions at all kinds of companies from current and former employees."
– *USA Today*

VAULT CAREER GUIDE TO
SOCIAL WORK

VAULT CAREER GUIDE TO
SOCIAL WORK

NATALIE WRIGHT, LMSW
AND THE STAFF OF VAULT

For information about permission to reproduce selections from this book, contact Vault Inc.,
150 W. 22nd St., 5th Floor, New York, NY 10011, (212) 366-4212.

Library of Congress CIP Data is available.

ISBN 10: 1-58131-454-x

ISBN 13: 978-1-58131-454-0

Printed in the United States of America

ACKNOWLEDGMENTS

Natalie Wright's acknowledgments:

Thank you to all of my social work friends and colleagues for providing materials for this book. Being able to take snippets from your lives has helped bring to life many of the concepts addressed in the book. Special thanks to Christine Horace, who has been an inspiration to me, and a true example of what a social worker is, through her dedication and genuine caring for others.

Vault's acknowledgments:

We are extremely grateful to Vault's entire staff for all their help in the editorial, production and marketing processes. Vault also would like to acknowledge the support of our investors, clients, employees, family, and friends. Thank you!

Table of Contents

Visit Vault at **www.vault.com** for insider company profiles, expert advice, career message boards, expert resume reviews, the Vault Job Board and more.

VAULT CAREER LIBRARY   ix

GETTING HIRED 33

Chapter 4: Education 35

Chapter 5: The Job Search 51

Chapter 6: Getting the Job You Want 57

Visit Vault at **www.vault.com** for insider company profiles, expert advice,
career message boards, expert resume reviews, the Vault Job Board and more.

VAULT CAREER LIBRARY

xi

Use the Internet's
MOST TARGETED
job search tools.

Vault Job Board

Target your search by industry, function, and experience
level, and find the job openings that you want.

VaultMatch Resume Database

Vault takes match-making to the next level: post your resume
and customize your search by industry, function, experience
and more. We'll match job listings with your interests and
criteria and e-mail them directly to your inbox.

VAULT
> the most trusted name in career information™

Introduction

Social work is a vast and dynamic field that offers boundless opportunities to grow and learn based on the world around you as well as the turns your own life takes. Depending on what area of social work you choose and with whom you decide to work with, your success will depend on your skills, both learned and innate. But your opportunities will only be limited by your own imagination. If you are looking for a career that is interesting, ever-changing and diverse, and having an abundance of options, social work may be for you. Good luck!

What is Social Work?

The goal of social work is to enhance the well-being of people, families and communities so that all can live to their fullest capacity. Most social workers enter this profession out of a desire to help improve people's lives through guidance, counseling and advocacy. They work directly with those facing life-threatening disease, disability, substance abuse or a social problem such as inadequate housing or unemployment. They work within communities, organizations and social, legal and educational systems to improve services and influence social policy. Their training in human development, personality theories, social relations and cultural norms allows them to evaluate people's needs and determine what resources are available to improve their conditions. Social workers are trained to look at the person in the context of his or her environment, including family composition, neighborhood and ethnic background, and its intersection with large society; in other words, they don't approach problems as though they occurred in a vacuum. Much of what social workers do is help people function the best they can in their environments.

Social workers work in a variety of settings, such as the traditional human service agencies serving children and families and in hospitals, but they can also be found in nontraditional arenas such as private businesses, politics and classrooms. In many settings, it is the social workers who are the first point of contact for a client, and it is their job to assess a client's needs and figure out what resources are available. In some positions, social workers provide individual and group counseling, staff supervision, case-management services and overall program guidance. In nontraditional settings such as private business, social workers work in employee assistance programs (EAPs), which help employees deal with stress, substance use, time

Visit Vault at **www.vault.com** for insider company profiles, expert advice, career message boards, expert resume reviews, the Vault Job Board and more.

VAULT CAREER LIBRARY

1

management and other issues that can affect work productivity. Still others decide that they would rather work for themselves and start private practices offering counseling and therapy to individuals, groups and families as well as private case consultation and supervision to other social workers.

The skills and experience gained from direct practice with individuals is sometimes transferred to a macro-level practice where one can influence the social policies that affect the most vulnerable in a community. Some become advisors to politicians; others conduct research on specific populations/issues, such as HIV. This research informs social policy, influences health care options and develops standard practices, often called best practices, which become the basis for service delivery to these populations.

Community-organizing social workers partner with community members-neighbors, local politicians and businesses-to open or save a community youth center, ask for more police presence in high crime areas or provide education and support for health care options and communicable diseases. These social workers often work within communities made up of the extremely poor, illegal immigrants and low-skilled workers to help improve their living, working and educational conditions.

Perhaps the newest area for social workers is trauma and disaster. Since the events of September 11th and through to Hurricane Katrina, social workers have been in the forefront as first responders because of their training in crisis intervention and ability to quickly analyze and evaluate the needs of those affected. Organizations such as the American Red Cross rely heavily on trained social workers to provide disaster mental health counseling; over 40 percent of their volunteers are professional social workers. Social workers provide direct services to victims, such as grief counseling, and bring together appropriate service providers and community resources to assist people in restoring their lives. The assessment skills social workers have are essential to providing these crisis-based services with compassion and efficiency.

THE SCOOP

The History of Social Work

Examples of social work practice can be found throughout history, generally flourishing during times when the growth of technology, politics or medicine outpaced that of society at large. In this chapter, we'll take a look at the evolution of social work and the various influences that made the field what it is today.

The British Influence

The Elizabethan Poor Laws of the 1600s tend to be cited as the benchmark of structured social work practices. This legislation imposed taxes on people in each parish or town to pay for their own poor. It also established apprentice programs for poor children, developed workhouses for dependent people and dealt harshly and punitively with able-bodied poor people. These punishments included the public whipping of orphan boys or vagabonds who stole or begged for money, and incarceration of adult men in workhouses. These laws set the standard for dealing with the poor and disadvantaged for over 200 years. The Plymouth colonists transplanted these poor laws from England to America, and went a step further, dividing the poor into two groups, the deserving sick and the undeserving offenders. The former group included widows, the disabled, orphans and thrifty old people. The latter were unmarried mothers, vagrants, the unemployed and the old without savings.

British almshouses or poorhouses began as early as the 10th century as an attempt at social welfare. These houses were set up to provide minimal care to the deserving sick and were mostly paid for by taxes from individual parishes or towns, not municipal dollars. People requested help from the community "Overseer of the Poor," an elected town official. If the need was great or likely to be long term, a person was sent to the poorhouse instead of being given immediate relief, such as money or food. Sometimes people were sent there even if they had not requested help from the Overseer of the Poor, usually when they were found guilty of begging in public or some other offense.

The Industrial Revolution

The late 1700s through the late 1800s, the time period between the beginning of the industrial revolution and the ending of the Civil War, marked the beginning of modern social work in the United States. As factories and mass production of goods multiplied, and agrarian-based jobs dried up, workers flocked to cities, which led to overcrowding, unemployment and poverty. Once in these newly industrialized cities, families quickly found out that survival, even at the lowest standards of poverty, required that every member of the family work, including children as young as six. It was not uncommon for children to work in factories 12 to14 hours per day with only a one-hour break, earning low to nonexistent wages.

As Americans began moving around the country and congregating where there were jobs, issues of culture and race emerged. Once the sparsely inhabited lands of the West were conquered, native peoples were moved onto reservations, their cultures and traditions altered due to their lack of connection with their transplanted homes and lands. When reconstruction began, freed black slaves faced discrimination in both Northern and Southern states, where they attempted to find work.

Charity begins in the home

As the industrial revolution continued, cities became more overcrowded, wages remained low, sanitation and general living conditions declined and immigration increased. Out of these circumstances grew an increased awareness of individual and community needs. In 1877, the first American Charity Organization Society (COS) of the United States was founded in Buffalo, New York. COS administered charitable programs and organized volunteer labor to help the needy, with the goal of restoring as much self-sufficiency and responsibility as an individual could manage. This society believed that simply offering aid in the form of money to the poor was not sufficient to alleviating the root causes of poverty. Instead they used techniques such as job skills training and taught budgeting skills to give the poor the tools they needed to elevate themselves. To this end, COS introduced the first formal training for social workers, who were called friendly visitors. For the most part, these visitors were young, wealthy, educated women, whose philosophy of "betterment of individuals and families, one by one" was met through teaching the poor and disadvantaged improved manners, health and hygiene. Visitors could also be found in schools, hospitals and other places the lower class depended on for assistance.

The practices of these individuals became the basis of the social casework that is taught and practiced today.

Settlement Houses

The settlement movement began in London around 1884, growing out of the Victorian concern about rising poverty. The idea was to have students and others connected with universities and/or wealth move into slum areas to live and work amongst neighborhood inhabitants. Shortly thereafter, Stanton Coit founded America's first settlement house, the Neighborhood Guild (later renamed University Settlement) on New York City's Lower East Side. In 1889, Jane Addams founded Hull House in Chicago, perhaps the most famous settlement house in the United States.

Settlement houses were not characterized by the services they provided, but rather by their philosophy, that the initiative to correct social ills should come from indigenous neighborhood leaders or organizations. Settlement workers, mostly college students and educated women, did not see themselves as dispensing charity in the form of money or services, but as working toward the general welfare of the community. With this strategy in mind, settlement houses moved issues of poverty from case to cause, meaning they used the problems of the individuals and families (case) in those neighborhoods to inform and improve social policies (cause). To do this, advocates studied the environmental causes of poverty as well as working, sanitation and sweatshop conditions, and explored ways to expand working opportunities for the poor. This research helped establish the juvenile court system, created widows' pension programs and promoted legislation prohibiting child labor. It introduced public health reforms like workplace safety standards for those working with arsenic, lead and noxious gases, and personal hygiene standards to reduce infections. Activism aided in the creation of health clinics, convalescent homes, playgrounds, nursing services and milk stations, which provided pure, sanitary milk to mothers with young children.

The end of settlement housing

The settlement house movement burgeoned until after WWI, when it seemed to lose its momentum. Some settlements disappeared as old residents left for the suburbs and new neighbors turned elsewhere to obtain services. On the whole, volunteerism declined. Professionally trained social workers and other human service workers took over the operation and administration of

Visit Vault at **www.vault.com** for insider company profiles, expert advice, career message boards, expert resume reviews, the Vault Job Board and more.

VAULT CAREER LIBRARY

7

settlements and they functioned mainly as community centers where recreational and basic social services were offered.

Today, settlement houses focus on areas such as immigration, youth services and housing for the homeless, mentally ill and the elderly. Founded in 1911, the United Neighborhood Centers of America continues to provide oversight and membership to approximately 156 settlement houses. UNCA provides its member houses with a way to link to others around the country to exchange ideas, missions and trends in populations.

War, Politics and Money

During World War I, social workers applied casework skills to treating soldiers with "shell shock." For the first time, social workers' skills were considered useful outside of impoverished communities. Post-World War I saw the beginnings of a shift in the populations social workers served. From the late 1920s through the 1960s, the middle-class became the primary beneficiaries of social policies, voluntary and public agencies. Also during this period, social activism declined and openly anti-welfare attitudes emerged. However, practice with individuals and families continued to flourish. By 1927 there were over 100 child guidance centers where interdisciplinary teams of psychiatrists, psychologists and social workers provided therapy to primarily middle-class clients on issues related to adjustment disorders, substance use and childhood trauma. The post-WWII period was also one of significant change in U.S. social welfare, highlighted by the establishment of the Department of Health, Education and Welfare (HEW) in 1953.

Social work continued to evolve through the difficult era of the 1970s, characterized by budget deficits and the stagnation of most social programs. As a result, there was a virtual freeze on aid to families with dependent children (AFDC) benefits or what is commonly called welfare, after 1973. Families relied on these benefits for assistance in purchasing nutritious foods and offsetting housing costs. The Carter administration then created a system called block grants, which provided the same amount of aid to states regardless of actual need, putting more populated states, such as New York, at a disadvantage to meet those needs with public dollars.

The 1980s bore the brunt of those 1970s policies and "Reaganomics" on America's disenfranchised. Fewer jobs led to soaring poverty and budget deficits meant not enough money to fund proper solutions. At the same time, new and more complex social problems were emerging, such as the crack cocaine epidemic, HIV/AIDS, domestic violence and homelessness. Social work demanded increased attention on developing effective management skills to maximize limited resources, as well as increased advocacy activities to persuade the government to pay more attention and spend more money on solutions.

In the 1990s, major policy developments had serious implications for the social work profession and the clients it served. Temporary assistance to needy families (TANF) was possibly the largest reform policy of that decade. This legislation placed a cap of five years for the amount of time a family could be on public assistance. After that, they could no longer receive welfare, housing rental assistance or food stamps, even if they remained needy. By 2000, social workers and social work agencies knew they would have to create innovative solutions for the perpetually needy. Some programs coped by developing or expanding their free food distribution services, applying for government and private grants to allow them to offer rent assistance to families facing eviction, and expanding clients' access to social workers to provide psychosocial support through this unstable time.

Evolution of Education

In 1898, a New York society of charitable organizations felt the need to become connected with a college to lend some professionalism to their image. They created the first philanthropy school, called the New York School of Philanthropy, which eventually became Columbia University School of Social Work. By 1901, other COS schools of philanthropy began operating across major U.S. cities and by 1919, there were 17 schools of social work affiliated as the Association of Training Schools of Professional Schools of Social Work, today's Council on Social Work Education (CSWE). This council provides standards of practice and teaching to all accredited schools of social work.

By 1920, there were five fields of practice in social work: family services, child services, medical, psychiatric and school social work. In the decade after World War II, social workers made efforts to enhance the field's professional status through the development of interdisciplinary doctoral training programs and the creation of core MSW curricula. The formation of CSWE in 1952 and the establishment of the National Association of Social Workers in 1955 further strengthened the status of the profession.

In the 1970s, on par with the changing social climate, the profession witnessed an increase in multicultural and gender awareness programs in

Visit Vault at **www.vault.com** for insider company profiles, expert advice, career message boards, expert resume reviews, the Vault Job Board and more.

VAULT CAREER LIBRARY

9

curricula, along with efforts to expand minority recruitment; the growth of multidisciplinary joint degree programs with schools of urban planning, public health, public policy, education and law; the recognition of the BSW as the entry-level professional degree; and the growth of private practice among social workers. And in the 1990s, due to the backlash on the poor and the need for creative solutions to poverty, NASW revised its code of ethics to make the pursuit of social justice an ethical imperative for those studying to become Social Workers, and CSWE required all schools to educate students about the skills necessary to work for economic and social justice.

Social Work Today

For over a century, the social work profession has matured and reinvented itself in response to economic and social changes, often in spite of society's inconsistent commitment to social welfare. Its primary mission continues to be advocating for the needs of the most vulnerable segments of society and improving their well-being. Social workers must develop a keen awareness of the impact of governmental policies, economic inequities and ideas related to culture, class, gender and race on individuals and communities, so that as society changes and needs arise, they will continue to play an integral role in enhancing the design and delivery of social services on every level, from community, to state and national to international.

What Do Social Workers Do?

CHAPTER 2

In this chapter, we will discuss what social workers do and where they do it. As with other professions, social work has many different levels within the profession in which individuals can work and advance based on their own goals and interests. Before choosing to pursue social work as a career, you must consider social work demographics and essential traits, as well as the distinction between professional and paraprofessional social work positions, and then look further into primary social work employers and roles in the field.

Social Workers: Who Are We?

According to NASW, there are over 600,000 professional social workers in the U.S. And according to the U.S. Bureau of Labor Statistics, in 2004 social workers held approximately 562,000 jobs, and employment is expected to rise faster than the average for all occupations through 2014, with hospitals, substance abuse, schools and private practice seeing the most increase. As people live longer, but not necessarily better quality lives, there will be a continued need for social workers to provide casework, advocacy, individual and family therapy.

In a study of approximately 2,000 members of NASW conducted in 2002 by the Practice Research Network (PRN), women make up 79 percent of all social workers, 91 percent of social workers have a Master's degree, 6 percent have doctoral degrees, and typically they have been in practice for 16 years. Ninety-two percent of NASW members are white or African-American, and 68% percent are between the ages of 43 and 62.

If one was to ask any of these social workers why they chose this field, the likely answer would hinge on a combination of their ideals, values and intrinsic qualities. This would have to be the answer, because it sure isn't for the money!

Visit Vault at **www.vault.com** for insider company profiles, expert advice, career message boards, expert resume reviews, the Vault Job Board and more.

VAULT CAREER LIBRARY   11

Essential Traits

Below are essential areas in which you should assess your own abilities/attitudes to help decide whether social work is right for you.

Confidentiality

Your ability to maintain a client's confidentiality is extremely important. It's not that social workers hide crimes, but they must maintain a client's confidences even when they think that it would be in their best interest to tell someone. For instance, if you conduct couples' counseling as well as individual counseling sessions, you'll probably often think that if you could bring in what each party had said in their individual counseling sessions, both parties would be able to better understand one another and progress in their relationship. But because of confidentiality, you are unable to do this, and you'll need to be creative in how you introduce information into the couples' sessions. Issues related to confidentiality range from this mild example to ones that bring the risk of legal consequences, such as in the area of HIV/AIDS. Confidentiality in relation to a person's HIV diagnosis is regulated by state and federal laws and the inability to adhere to these rules could mean a trip to court for you.

Trustworthiness

Increasingly, many in the field are not members of the communities they serve which can make it tough to build trust. Among certain immigrant, religious and minority groups, whose experience in the United States has been marred by transgressions, violence and discrimination, professionals must convey that they can be trusted with personal information and that they are truly committed to working together toward a solution. So, if you are not a part of the community you are serving, or if you are of a different race, religion or gender than the clients or community you work with, you must be able to show that you are trustworthy and sincere in your desire to assist them in reaching their goals.

Sincerity

You'll need to work with a nonjudgmental attitude, offering all of your clients the same level of service regardless of your feelings about them or their current issue. While providing a service, you should be aware of your facial expressions, mannerisms and how you are addressing the issue. If clients pick up on your disapproval of their lifestyle, they may not return for services.

Empathy, sympathy and pity

As you enter the field you will find that many professionals began as clients, or that otherwise well-intentioned people will join the field to "help the poor people." Although neither of these groups is misguided in its spirit, both types do need to keep their personal views in check. Using empathy is a cornerstone of social work education and practice. When you empathize with someone, you are able to put yourself in his or her shoes or understand his or her feelings about a particular situation based on your own experiences. For instance, although you may never have been homeless, likely you do understand how it would feel to not belong anywhere and have no control over your own space.

But when you sympathize, you are removing the professional boundary and replacing what your client is feeling with your own feelings, based on your experience of the same situation. Because of this, you will not be able to offer objective guidance to this client. And expressing pity to a client won't work. Most clients do not want to have to see a social worker at all, so when they do, they want to be seen as a whole person experiencing a situation, not a situation cloaked as a person.

Prioritize, Partialize, Refer

This is a good mantra to remember, especially on those really tough days. What it means is that you need to figure out what your client came in for and what you can provide, then prioritize those needs and then partialize or break them down into smaller, more manageable parts. The stuff that you cannot help with gets referred to a person or program that can.

Visit Vault at **www.vault.com** for insider company profiles, expert advice, career message boards, expert resume reviews, the Vault Job Board and more.

V/\ULT CAREER LIBRARY

13

Professional and Paraprofessional

Generally, social work positions are divided into two main areas, professional and paraprofessional social work.

A paraprofessional is generally classified as a case aide, a technician or a peer. These positions tend to rely more on personal attributes like life experience and personality than level of education. Persons in these positions usually perform basic counseling or provide concrete services that do not require clinical skills. For instance, in a homeless shelter, the case aide may be the person who shows new residents to their rooms and acquaints them with shelter rules and regulations. Aides would then turn over paperwork to social workers or other clinical staff for a more complete assessment of needs and ongoing care, and would have limited interaction with shelter residents going forward. During overnight and weekend shifts, aides are usually in charge of the shelter, with a director on call for backup. Aides may also help prepare meals and provide limited child care and security duties.

Other duties paraprofessionals may perform include determining preliminary eligibility for government-sponsored welfare programs, facilitating support groups as a peer educator in a HIV/AIDS program, accompanying clients to public assistance offices or medical appointments, and making follow-up calls to clients about their health, housing search or other goals they may have set.

Many programs also hire paraprofessionals as case workers or case managers who provide concrete services, as opposed to therapeutic interventions. Places a paraprofessional may find work include hospitals, nonprofits and municipal human service departments such as child protection agencies and public assistance offices.

Those considered professional social workers have, at minimum, a four-year undergraduate degree. Below we'll look at major categories of professional social work jobs.

As we will discuss in chapter three, the government, nonprofits and hospitals provide the majority of jobs in social work. Be familiar with the setting in which you'd like to practice and the population you wish to practice with, because it will determine the type of education, field practice (internship) or other preemployment opportunities you may want to take advantage of. This is not to say that you are locked into any particular setting, but the better informed your decision, the more successful and satisfied you will be.

Family and Children Services

Social workers in this role work to improve the social and psychological functioning of children and their families to maximize the family's well-being. Some social workers assist single parents in locating child care and dealing with parenting alone; they may arrange adoptions for people who want to adopt and for those who want to have their children adopted; and they help find foster homes for neglected, abandoned or abused children.

Case study

When Billy arrived at school, his teacher noticed a large bruise on his shoulder, just above his shirt collar. When his teacher asked where the bruise came from, Billy said that his mother hit him last night because he would not eat his vegetables. Because all teachers are mandated to report child abuse, Billy's teacher contacted the local administration for children's services. Later that week, a social worker came to Billy's house to assess him and his sister for child abuse. When the worker arrived, she found Billy's mother had been drinking all day and was not able to properly care for her children.

The social worker then recommended that Billy and his sister be placed in foster care while their mother receives help for her drinking. The social worker began by locating a substance and alcohol use program for Billy's mother to help her stop drinking, give her some insight into why she drinks and what triggers her to drink. The social worker then mandated that Billy's mom attend parenting classes to learn about appropriate discipline, healthy parenting techniques and skills on stress management.

To find a foster family, the social worker first attempted to locate family members willing to take in both children. When that did not work, she has them placed with a prescreened foster family or into a group home until the family can be reunited.

Social workers in family and children's services will unfortunately see many Billys during the course of their work. Since the goal in this field is to ensure the health and well-being of children, sometimes they have to make tough decisions about what is best for the child, like an out-of-home placement until the family can better support the child's needs. Sometimes, in more extreme

Visit Vault at **www.vault.com** for insider company profiles, expert advice, career message boards, expert resume reviews, the Vault Job Board and more.

VAULT CAREER LIBRARY   **15**

cases of abuse and neglect, social workers have to work with the police, courts and lawyers to protect the child.

Commonly, social workers in this line will work for child welfare agencies, Child Protective Services (CPS) or family preservation agencies, typically operated by private nonprofits or state and local governments. Some examples are adoption agencies, foster care agencies and group homes, as well as public and private child welfare organizations. Private agencies, such as Catholic Charities, are generally operated by nonprofits or religious groups and funded by government grants, private donations or money from private foundations specifically set up to fund child welfare programs.

In agencies such as the Administration for Children's Services (ACS) in New York City, where abuse and neglect are the main focus, social workers investigate allegations that place children at risk for harm and then make recommendations on how to deal with the allegations. These may range from family counseling to the removal of children or parents from the home and, in more extreme cases, criminal charges. Social workers are responsible for appropriately documenting their findings, as they may be used in court hearings for custody or criminal charges. The emotional state of the abused person, condition of the home, involvement of drugs or alcohol, physical evidence of the abuse and reports from family, friends and medical personnel are examples of the type of information necessary to make a determination of a case.

In addition to abuse and neglect services, these social workers also focus on areas such as family communication, adjustment to changes within families, such as divorce or marriage, and they can also provide marriage counseling to couples.

School Social Work

Public and private schools from elementary through to college employ social workers to address issues such as truancy, teenage pregnancy, suicide and mental illness. They may be called upon to advise teachers on coping with disruptive students, and they also teach workshops to classes on topics such as self-esteem, sexuality and violence in the home. Parents and social workers combine efforts when family life disruptions, such as death, divorce or even the birth of a new sibling has an effect on the student's learning.

Case study

Sally's grades have been declining since the winter break, and she no longer sits with her friends at lunch. Sally's teacher is concerned that there may be something going on at home or in school that is affecting Sally's academic performance and has isolated her. Sally's teacher brings her concerns to the school's social worker for help. The social worker listens to the teacher's concerns and asks some of Sally's other teachers about her performance. All of Sally's teachers note some change in her demeanor and performance.

The school social worker calls Sally into her office, talks to her about her teachers' concerns and asks if anything has changed at home or in school recently. After some time, Sally reveals that the "cool" kids in school are bullying her because she is overweight compared to some of her classmates. The social worker counsels Sally on self-esteem and body image for the rest of the school year, and intervenes with the students who were bullying her, contacting their teachers and parents to notify them of the situation so they can help keep Sally safe from the bullying. The social worker also involves Sally's parents, alerting them to the problem and offering them suggestions on how to deal with the issue at home, referring them to family counseling so they can support Sally through this difficult time.

At the end of the year, Sally was able to bring up her grades but decides she would rather transfer to another school than come back to her current one.

Today, instances of bullying have become much more common and are being taken very seriously in schools. News coverage of bullying is pervasive, from how it is affecting children's self-images and school performance, to the violent outbursts that result when the pressure becomes unbearable. School social workers team with parents, teachers, school administrators and students to help ensure that the school environment is healthy for all students.

In this field, the family and other people/programs the student may be involved in are often called upon to increase support for the student. These "teams" help students deal with learning disabilities, changes in the home such as the death or divorce of a parent, emotional and mental health problems, domestic violence and poverty issues. School social workers' offices also provide students with a safe place to just talk. In some cases, a student may not have a dire problem, but sometimes just wants to vent to

Visit Vault at **www.vault.com** for insider company profiles, expert advice, career message boards, expert resume reviews, the Vault Job Board and more.

VAULT CAREER LIBRARY

17

someone they know will listen. School social workers may also serve as quasi-guidance counselors, impressing upon students how important it is to stay in school and to do well.

In head start centers for preschool-aged children, school-based social workers evaluate and provide early interventions for students who may have learning disorders or other issues that could impede their ability to learn and function well in mainstream schooling. At primary and secondary schools with adolescents, the focus is on disruptive behavior, family and interpersonal relationships, signs of abuse, mental disorders and other factors that can contribute to low achievement in classes. Social workers in special education schools and counseling centers geared towards school-aged children work intensively to help children and families understand the disability and give the child the tools necessary to live a full life in spite of handicaps.

Medical Social Work

Medical social workers provide individuals and families with the psychosocial support needed to cope with chronic, acute or terminal illnesses, such as Alzheimer's, cancer, AIDS and other medical conditions that cause a disruption to regular life. They also advise family caregivers on the prognosis of the ill person's condition and how to best care for the person at home, or they'll recommend nursing home or hospice care when necessary. They provide counseling to patients on what to expect as their condition progresses, to alleviate some of the anxiety of not knowing what will happen next. And social workers help plan for patients' needs after discharge from hospitals or rehabilitation centers by arranging for at-home services, from meals-on-wheels to oxygen equipment.

Case study

Wilson, 73, has been in the Karson Rehabilitation Center for approximately three months after having his left leg partially amputated due to a vein blockage. While there, Wilson has received intensive physical therapy and guidance on how to use his new prosthetic leg. Wilson is now ready for discharge and has an appointment to see the social worker for discharge planning. The social worker, Catherine, talks to Wilson about his expectations for when he returns home and what assistance he may need. They decide that a removable ramp will be needed on the front steps so he can use his wheelchair to get in and out of the house. Additionally, Catherine arranges for safety bars to be installed in the bathtub and along the walls in the house and contacts a visiting nurse service for in-home care related to Wilson's activities of daily living (ADL) such as bathing, dressing and cleaning his wound site, and to provide ongoing rehabilitation therapy. She also suggests that Wilson and his wife attend counseling sessions to work through any changes in their relationship that may result from the amputation.

Without the intervention of the social worker, Wilson could have been discharged without the proper tools needed to make his homecoming successful. Wilson may have lost his mobility and sense of autonomy altogether without the wheelchair ramp, which would help him in coming and going as he pleased. The rehab specialist who came to the house made it possible for Wilson to maneuver around his home and outside with his prosthetic leg. And the counselor gave Wilson and his wife a safe place to talk about their difficulties and changes in their relationship since the amputation. Without all of the pieces in place, Wilson could have faced a very difficult time readjusting to his home.

Medical social workers can be assigned cases from doctors, or can be requested by patients or family members. In cases where patients are not able to make appropriate medical decisions about their care, a social worker may be called upon to explain this to the family and help them decide who should make the decisions. If a baby is born and there are multiple problems that require additional long- or short-term care, a social worker will talk with family members to determine what services are needed and where the family can go to receive them. In ERs, social workers are made available to women who come in with injuries from sexual assault and domestic violence. These professionals listen to the victims and help them take next steps, whether that is police intervention, counseling or referral to a shelter.

Medical social workers can also practice in nursing homes with elderly or disabled residents. Here they provide much of the same duties as visiting services, but also may be in charge of recreational and social skills-building activities. They may also provide education and counseling to family members for a patient's illness and prognosis.

Visit Vault at www.vault.com for insider company profiles, expert advice, career message boards, expert resume reviews, the Vault Job Board and more.

VAULT CAREER LIBRARY

19

Mental Health Social Work

Mental health social workers work in inpatient settings such as psychiatric hospitals, or in the community at therapeutic centers or community mental health programs that provide counseling and medication monitoring for patients outside of the hospital. Social workers in these centers often work closely with other providers, medical doctors, case managers and family members to ensure that each is aware of the clients' treatment and their cooperation in the treatment.

Case study

Kenneth works in a community mental health program as the supervising social worker. Throughout the day, Kenneth interacts with many patients to evaluate their level of mental functioning and safety to themselves and the community. Today, Gerry comes in and says that his voices have returned, and they have told him that he should stop taking his medications. This immediately alarms Kenneth because of Gerry's history of violence when not taking his medications properly. Kenneth assesses Gerry for recent violence and finds that two days ago he punched a hole in his bedroom wall because he was unable to find something in his bedroom. This alerted Kenneth to the fact that Gerry may have already stopped taking his medications. Kenneth excuses himself from the counseling room and asks the front desk person to contact emergency services for Gerry. When Kenneth returns to the room, he informs Gerry of what he has just done and explains it was for his own good. Gerry is upset at first, but because he trusts Kenneth, he agrees to go with the emergency services when they arrive. Gerry will most likely be admitted to the local psychiatric hospital for observation and his medication regime will be restarted. Once he is ready for discharge, the hospital will contact Kenneth so he and Gerry can continue their counseling sessions.

Working in the community brings in two kinds of clients, the individual and the community itself. Kenneth's goal is to get Gerry the best help he can. But it is also to keep the community safe from Gerry's violent outbursts. If Kenneth had not laid the groundwork of building trust with Gerry, he may have run out of the clinic as soon as he heard that emergency services were on their way.

Mental health social workers provide a myriad of services to individuals and families experiencing or affected by mental illness. They may provide group and individual therapy addressing mental illness symptoms and treatment options for patients and their families. They work in agencies that provide respite care for parents or other caregivers, allowing them to take a break from caring for the patient so they do not become too overwhelmed. They may diagnose and provide treatment recommendations for patients in psychiatric hospitals. As in Kenneth's case, they provide crisis intervention by removing the patients from the community to protect them. They may also train patients in activities of daily living (ADL), such as proper hygiene, cooking, cleaning and shopping.

Similar to a medical social worker, mental health social workers need to be aware of prevailing psychiatric disorders, such as schizophrenia, depression and bi-polar disorder, as well as their symptomology, treatments and signs of decompensation, or deterioration. In many community mental health programs, drug use is also an issue that has to be contended with, so being aware of drug interactions is important to this work. When a client who has a history of drug use comes into your office and you suspect he is using again, being able to differentiate psychiatric symptoms from drug-induced behavior is important to deciding what type of care you will give.

When working in this field, you may struggle with the dual role of community protector and patient advocate. Many clients are harmless to the community when not taking their medications, but the mandate of a mental health social worker is to ensure clients adhere to their regiments. When a client cites sleep disturbance, dry mouth, a drowsy or cloudy feeling and frequent urination as reasons why they stopped their medications, it is easy to understand their frustration, but as a clinician, a mental health social worker must educate clients on the benefits of taking their medications, which may range from decreased hallucinations, better interpersonal relationships and more normal sleep and wake cycles in spite of their grievances. The underlying presumption of this work is that if stable on medications, most mentally ill patients can live productive normal lives.

Substance Abuse Social Work

Social workers in the substance use and addiction field are trained to treat clients holistically, taking into account a person's physical environment, family support system, spiritual beliefs and cultural attitudes, along with the addiction. Traditionally, substance use counseling was handled by people with CASAC certification (credentialed alcoholism and substance abuse

Visit Vault at **www.vault.com** for insider company profiles, expert advice, career message boards, expert resume reviews, the Vault Job Board and more.

VAULT CAREER LIBRARY

21

counselor), but more recently social workers have been filling these roles because of their more specialized training and holistic approach to treatment.

This field is a good example of how the diverse and flexible skills of social workers can adapt to a number of different issues. Many in the substance abuse field only treat the actual substance use, meaning they work with people only to decrease or eliminate their use of drugs. The holistic approach used by social workers targets not only a person's drug use, but also aims at working out what may have caused the person to begin using or to be unable to stop. Social workers understand that unless these underlying issues, which might range from childhood sexual abuse or domestic violence to feelings of inadequacy or peer pressure, are attended to, a person may never successfully stop using drugs.

Case study

Danielle has been attending Narcotics Anonymous meetings for the past six months and has not used heroin in this time. Recently, Danielle lost her mother, with whom she was very close. Since then, Danielle has not been attending meetings as regularly, and has begun hanging out with some old friends who knew her mother for support through this time. But these old friends are also people Danielle used drugs with in the past. At first, Danielle is able to resist the urge to use and her friends seem to respect her recovery. But on the day of her mother's funeral, Danielle could no longer fight the urge and begins shooting heroin again. Within two months, Danielle loses her job, her apartment and uses up all of her savings on drugs. One day, while walking downtown to get more drugs, Danielle passes the place where she used to attend the NA meetings. An attendee recognizes Danielle and realizes that she had begun using again. This attendee engages Danielle in conversation and convinces her to seek treatment for her addiction at an outpatient methadone maintenance program.

The program's social worker, Ferdinand, trained in substance use and addiction, helps Danielle understand her addiction and what triggers or situations may lead to her using heroin. Ferdinand also encourages Danielle to begin working and restoring the life she had prior to her relapse. With this help, Danielle is able to find a new job and obtain an apartment. She has been on methadone for several months and now feels ready to decrease the dosage and eventually stop taking it.

Social workers may encounter people like Danielle in a variety of different settings, from a shelter to a clinic. Among Danielle's issues are her substance use, homelessness, lack of employment, grief over the loss of her mother and lack of a healthy support system. She could have come into a homeless shelter, substance use clinic, employment office or an open grief and loss group for any of her issues, but without also addressing her substance use not much progress would have been made in any of these other areas. The fields of mental health and substance use are more linked these days than ever. In recent years the terms MICA, CAMI, "dually diagnosed" and "double trouble" have become popular to describe those who have a mental illness and use drugs. Specialists in this field are trained to make differential diagnoses in which they decide what behaviors, thought patterns or symptoms are a part of the mental illness versus the drug use. When treating this population, clinicians must treat drug use and mental illness simultaneously, as both are seen as the prevailing illness. Being aware of drug interactions between street drugs, such as heroin, and psychiatric medications is important not only for treatment purposes, but also for possible fatal complications.

Education, monitoring and behavior modification are major responsibilities in these positions. Educating clients on the possible harmful effects of street drugs and fatal medical interactions with their psychiatric medications is essential, as is monitoring the continuing use of psychiatric medications and the possibility of destructive behavior while high, such as violence or high risk sex. Helping clients to modify their behaviors to reduce potential harm from the drug use, such as only using on weekends, modifying or reducing the amount of drugs used at a single sitting or binge and not spending all of their food money on drugs are some examples of this.

Clinical Social Work

Clinical social workers rely on a variety of therapeutic theories and tools to help individuals, couples, families and groups with mental, behavioral and emotional disorders, from eating issues to depression to personality disorders. Unlike other areas of practice, clinical social workers are defined more by how they work than where and for whom. For instance, clinical social workers practice in schools, mental health agencies, private practice and community-based organizations, whereas those who practice school social work are only found in schools or school-based settings.

Visit Vault at **www.vault.com** for insider company profiles, expert advice, career message boards, expert resume reviews, the Vault Job Board and more.

VAULT CAREER LIBRARY   **23**

Case study

Martha is a 40-year-old woman who describes herself as having felt "down" for the past three months. Martha contacts her job's employee assistance program (EAP) for help and is referred to Pat, a clinical social worker, for therapy. During the first session, Pat asks Martha a series of questions related to her feelings of hopelessness, her satisfaction with her life and disturbances in her eating and sleeping habits. Martha explains that she has been feeling very hopeless lately, does not find enjoyment in many of her normal activities and has been oversleeping and overeating. Additionally, Martha reveals that she has thought about "disappearing" and that if she were not around, "no one would care." Pat determines that Martha is experiencing depression and over the next several weeks continues regular therapy sessions to try to recognize the cause of Martha's depression and help relieve it.

After several sessions, Pat and Martha decide that Martha's depression set in when her teenage son left for college and she was left home alone. Together, Pat and Martha decide that Martha should join an empty nest support group for parents in similar situations. Once she joins the group, Martha meets other parents who had felt the same way she did, and she begins socializing outside of the group with some of the other mothers. Through this socializing and her sessions with Pat, Martha's depression subsides and she is able to find joy in her life again.

According to NASW, clinical social workers are the largest group of professionally trained mental health providers in the United States, supplying more than half of counseling and therapy services. Clinical social workers have either a master's or doctorate in social work with a concentration in clinical course work, supervised graduate clinical field internship and at least two years of postgraduate supervised clinical social work employment.

Is Social Work for You?

So do you have what it takes? First things first: do you like people? If not, then this is not the career for you. Fundamentally, social work is about helping people. Even if you decide that working in policy is for you, you still need to have an understanding of the people who will be affected by the policy you seek to change. That may require focus group work, participant research or actually working in the field or with a specific population until you have enough experience to be hired to work on policy issues as an "expert" with that population.

But just getting along with people is not enough. Social workers are often the "mediators" between groups, individuals or communities. Having the skills to deal with the angry, disenfranchised and stubborn is essential.

Another core quality is the ability to function in dysfunction. Many of social workers' clients are seeing them during the worst times in their lives, and are relying on social workers to sort them out and make them whole again. Whether the issue has to do with family problems, spousal abuse, housing inadequacy or lack of money, you may find yourself at a loss and want to throw your hands in the air. While this is a perfectly reasonable reaction (behind closed doors and away from your clients), you still need to be able to assist these client through their issues.

The social worker's dilemma

For example, your client may be receiving rental subsidies from the government. Many of these programs now require families to pay an increasing percentage of their rent out of their own pockets, whereas in the past they were not required to pay any portion from their own earnings. If a person is receiving a subsidy, it generally means they are not earning enough money to cover their household and family expenses as well as pay the rent. Additionally, many people on these subsidy programs do not earn enough money to cover many of their basic necessities and may also be on welfare. If your client begins making too much money (enough to cover the rent increase) he will likely be kicked off of welfare due to that income increase. This will then make him unable to pay his rent, ineligible for welfare assistance and potentially homeless as a result. So where do you start? Do you suggest your client not work or advance in his current job in order to keep the subsidy? Do you try to find money to help with the rent on a one-time basis? Then what about the other months the rent won't be paid?

The best answer to this dilemma is to remember what your role/job function is, and be clear about what you can and cannot provide this family. As mentioned earlier, "prioritize, partialize, refer" will help make this and similar situations much more manageable. One of the biggest mistakes social workers make is in trying to be all things to all people. Social workers may encourage clients to observe boundaries, but must remember to assert their own as well. Learning to be clear about what you can and cannot do, based on your job function will be helpful not only to you in terms of being clear

Visit Vault at **www.vault.com** for insider company profiles, expert advice, career message boards, expert resume reviews, the Vault Job Board and more.

VAULT CAREER LIBRARY   25

about your responsibilities, but also to your client. He'll be less likely to be disappointed in you when things do not work in his favor, and place that disappointment where it belongs, on the system that failed him.

Taking stock of your personal beliefs and values is also important. Unlike plumbers or handymen who can carry tool boxes filled with everything they need, social workers only have their teachings and instincts to guide them through the work. Although you can't prepare for everything, being aware of the core issues that affect your ability to do the work are important. For instance, one young social worker we'll call Tony had strong beliefs about drug use among African-Americans (a community he was a member of), and he was assigned to a substance use program for his first-year placement. He received some training in substance use counseling prior to his first day, and thought he would be ok with it. But by the middle of that first day he had decided that he could not return the next day because it went against his own values about drug use. This social work student recognized that based on who he is, he could not provide competent services to this population and removed himself from that environment. This is not always an option, but particularly in social work, if workers understand themselves, they will be better equipped to deal with these situations when they arise-and they will arise. In most professional settings, social workers will have to contend with hot button issues such as abortion, interracial relationships, domestic violence, child abuse and poverty, and will have to figure out how to effectively work with clients around these issues. Some introspection on these types of issues is necessary before considering a career in social work.

Where Do Social Workers Work?

CHAPTER 3

The options social workers have in terms of employers are limitless, since the skills and abilities social workers have lend themselves to an infinite number of industries. Where you work is as much determined by your own desires as by your training. In this chapter we'll take a look at some of the most frequent employers of social workers.

The role of policy change

It is worth mentioning that opportunities in social work can expand or contract based on society's current concerns, which can fluctuate as quickly as fashion trends. The past decade has seen increasingly conservative government policies in relation to spending on social welfare programs and education, and an emphasis on the concept of morally correct government. The poor, uneducated, low-skilled, immigrant and young people of America have been negatively affected by some of these policies, which limit their access to necessary services. Social workers, too, find themselves affected by changes in policy, as funding may limit the number of jobs available and government ideas about the type of programming necessary for these populations may be contradictory to what social workers believe is effective and necessary.

The recent federal ban on abortion is an example of how government policies affect social work. Whether or not a social worker agrees with the ban, in limiting or restricting a client's options in response to an unplanned pregnancy, this kind of enactment also affects the social worker's ability to help clients make choices for themselves. Policy changes like this one can leave practitioners and clients with limited options, and sometimes will even shut down programs if this was their sole purpose for existence.

Government

Local, state and federal governments offer many opportunities for social workers to engage directly with clients as well as indirectly though policy work, research and program administration. Government services cover a wide range of issues, including public health, child and family services, homelessness, mental health, poverty and the law. For the most part, these

Visit Vault at **www.vault.com** for insider company profiles, expert advice, career message boards, expert resume reviews, the Vault Job Board and more.

V/\ULT CAREER LIBRARY   27

programs focus on meeting the basic needs of people such as food, shelter, safety and medical care by administering public welfare benefits (food stamps and cash assistance), coordinating entrance to homeless shelters and determining eligibility for Medicaid or Medicare health insurance.

A social worker in this field might work as a field interviewer for the local department of health, investigating the asthma rates in neighborhoods where there are limited medical resources and health care options. Other examples of government positions include social workers at municipal homeless shelters, an executive director in a state office of domestic violence prevention, or a social worker at the local public high school. Social workers may work with a city's district attorney's office to interview children who have been victims or witnesses of a crime, provide short-term counseling and referrals to rape victims or provide expert testimony on a person's mental stability at the time of or as a result of a crime. As an analyst, a social worker may track trends in homelessness to pinpoint root causes of indigence or determine why a particular segment of the population is showing an increase in homelessness. These statistics can be used to develop preventative programs; if lack of affordable housing is determined to be a major cause of homelessness, an analyst can propose an increase in the number of apartments available to a city's low-income residents.

Public health social workers strive to improve the health of individuals, families and communities through a holistic approach to illness. They perform this work as part of teams involving doctors, epidemiologists, dentists and others who focus on the health of populations. Hospitals, county health departments, the Center for Disease Control and Prevention (CDC), the National Institutes of Health (NIH) and the Substance Abuse and Mental Health Services Administration (SAMHSA) are a few of the more well-known public health-related government agencies that employ social workers.

In these positions, social workers provide teens, adults, children, infants, the elderly and entire vulnerable populations the psychosocial (emotional, social, mental and spiritual) support needed to cope with chronic, acute or terminal illnesses, such as Alzheimer's and HIV/AIDS. This support can include counseling both to help people deal with stress and loss, and to encourage them to participate in healthy activities such as sports, support groups and to adhere to medical advice or treatment.

Public health social workers also work with people who abuse drugs or have mental illness and around social issues such as teen pregnancy and obesity. Services include educating and advising individuals and caregivers about the particular illness or condition they are experiencing so they may make more informed decisions about their care and be better able to protect themselves and the community if they suffer from a communicable illness. Social workers may work with entire communities to evaluate the quality of services that are already in place and recommend changes or improvements. When outbreaks of unusual or particularly harmful diseases occur, social workers are called upon to gather background information on those afflicted as well as provide counseling and education to the community to prevent further infections.

Not-for-profit

Not-for-profit, sometimes shortened to nonprofit, refers to an organization established for purposes other than profit making. Major nonprofit employers of social workers include agencies like Good Shepherd Services, Salvation Army, UNICEF, the Boys and Girls Club, the YMCA and The American Red Cross, where social workers range in position from the highest-level management to the person greeting you at the door. Most social service agencies that are not government-administered are nonprofits. The mission of most nonprofits is to alleviate or ameliorate some social ill, such as homelessness, poverty, hunger, violence or disease.

The funding for these agencies may come from government grants (but are not directed by government), private donations and foundations established to alleviate a particular health condition or social ill. Nonprofit agencies offer a wealth of job opportunities for social workers, from front-line to managerial, in many different fields, including youth services, health care, crime prevention, residential programs for teens in foster care, and working with the developmentally disabled, mentally ill, physically ill or immigrant populations. According to the Bureau of Labor Statistics, employment in nonprofits is only expected to increase.

Public Policy

Local, state and federal government, as well as nonprofit and private businesses, hires policy social workers as lobbyists, analysts, evaluators and researchers to determine causes of certain social ills and propose possible remedies, much like research-oriented social workers we'll discuss later. Social workers in this field address problems such as child abuse, homelessness, substance abuse, poverty, mental illness, violence,

Visit Vault at **www.vault.com** for insider company profiles, expert advice, career message boards, expert resume reviews, the Vault Job Board and more.

VAULT CAREER LIBRARY   **29**

unemployment and racism, working to improve systems to better conditions for the people affected. Social workers analyze policies, programs and regulations to determine what solutions are most effective for a given problem. They identify social problems, study needs and related issues, conduct research, propose legislation and suggest alternative approaches or new programs. They may foster coalitions of groups with similar interests and develop interorganizational networks. On a daily basis, this often means analyzing census data and legislation, drafting position papers, testifying at public hearings, working with the media, talking with policymakers, and lobbying elected and appointed officials. Their tasks may also involve raising funds, writing grants or conducting demonstration projects. Often, social workers are the directors of organizations that do this work.

Work on one issue may take many months or years, and change is often incremental. But work in the policy and planning field earns social workers the satisfaction of knowing they are pressing our society to improve the quality of life for all of its members.

Hospitals

All hospitals have social workers on staff, especially specialized hospitals and rehabilitation centers. These include hospitals for special surgery such as orthopedics, hospice centers and short- or long-term rehabilitation centers in which social workers counsel patients on their diagnosis, recovery issues, adjustment back to normal life, or coping with the loss of a family member.

Corporate Industry

KPMG, Deloitte & Touche and Ernst & Young are a few of the corporate consulting companies winning contracts from government and nonprofit organizations for technical assistance in improving the delivery of social services, through team-development, training and administration. These companies look to hire master's level social workers to develop and deliver training on topics including organizational development, conflict resolution, help with technology solutions, policies and procedures tailored to the agencies' specific needs, and clinical guidance to other social workers. Because of social workers' specialized educational and experiential training in terms of the staff, clients and issues nonprofits face, they give these companies a unique edge in this type of setting, which increases the effectiveness of the training. To be successful in this field, it is important to have good analytical, strategic planning, presentation and writing skills. Seeking internships in corporations is an important step in acquiring this kind of position upon graduation.

Other Settings

Forensic social work

The National Organization of Forensic Social Work defines this practice as the application of social work to questions and issues relating to the law and legal systems. Those who specialize in this field perform duties such as evaluation of people and events for criminal and civil litigation. These social workers talk to children who are victims of sexual abuse to evaluate their stories and make recommendations that the courts use in determining the depth of trauma to the child and the punishment for the offender. These evaluations are written in language easily understood by the court system and not necessarily by traditionally trained social workers. Testifying in court as expert witnesses in abuse cases, determining the ability of a child victim to testify, evaluating and treating law enforcement personnel for workforce suitability, and training criminal justice personnel in working with juvenile offenders are a few of the duties of this field.

International social work

This field offers social workers the opportunity to travel as well as work directly with people from other countries to help enhance their quality of life. UNICEF, the United Nations (UN) and Mercy Corps, among others, provide opportunities for social workers to do paid work outside of the U.S. Most of the employment opportunities involve some work with health care, e.g. HIV/AIDS, tuberculosis, chicken pox or malaria, but there are also environmental, agricultural and community organizing programs. Most of these agencies' missions in some form are to alleviate poverty, suffering, oppression and enhance country infrastructure. The Peace Corps and the Red Cross also offer opportunities for international work, including providing shelter, food and clear water in war-torn regions such as Darfur and Iraq.

While in school you can declare international social work as your interest and obtain an internship that allows you to either work with one of these organizations in the U.S. in a more administrative/planning capacity, or travel abroad to do the direct service work.

Visit Vault at **www.vault.com** for insider company profiles, expert advice, career message boards, expert resume reviews, the Vault Job Board and more.

V∧ULT CAREER LIBRARY   **31**

Trauma disaster and emergency preparedness

Within the past decade alone, there have been a number of natural and manmade disasters that have caused unprecedented suffering. From September 11th to the Indian Ocean tsunami to Hurricane Katrina to the Virginia Tech shootings, voluntary aid organizations have been on the frontlines helping people rebuild their lives. The Red Cross, Mercy Corps, Americares, America's Second Harvest and the United Way are a few of the organizations providing needed services. Social workers in this field provide everything from the crisis intervention directly following the event to long-term solutions months and years later. Providing food and blankets, setting up clean water stations, talking survivors through their ordeal, engaging community resources to donate supplies and services to the affected and facilitating meetings to help communities heal are among the duties here. Once the disaster is over, social workers in emergency preparedness help to put measures in place so that in the event some similar situation occurs, the community, government officials and aid programs are ready to respond quickly. Although this is a relatively new area for social work, social workers' training in helping individuals deal with small-scale disasters such as death or disease, makes them well-suited to working with entire communities when large-scale disasters occur.

Growth Areas

There is expected to be a strong demand for substance abuse social workers over the next ten years and more, as drug users are increasingly being placed into treatment programs instead of being sentenced to prison. The criminal justice and correctional systems are increasingly requiring substance abuse treatment as a condition of sentencing or probation. As treatment programs become more widespread, demand will increase for social workers who can assist drug users on the road to recovery.

Another area where growth is expected is among social workers and employers who focus on the elderly or in the area of gerontology. Although hospitals are keeping patients for shorter periods of time, home health care is growing, in keeping with the increased demand of seniors who can live at home, but need additional support to do so. Additionally, the growing number of nursing homes, retirement communities and assisted living facilities is creating a wealth of opportunities for social workers in this field.

GETTING HIRED

Education

How do you learn to be an effective social worker? What type of social worker do you want to be? What population will you work with? How long do you want to be in school? And finally, what do you need to do to get hired as a social worker? This section will help you answer these questions, and more.

Undergraduate Options

Many a social work career began with a bachelor's degree in sociology, psychology or other related field. If you're haphazardly taking courses that look interesting based on their description, along the way you may realize that you enjoy and are interested in how people think and the dynamics of group behavior; the next thing you know, what began as a random path has turned into a deliberate and successful career.

Paraprofessionals in social work generally don't have a bachelor's degree, but do have at least a two-year associates' degree and the personality and life experience well suited to these entry-level positions.

Bachelor's degree

Professional social work positions require at least a bachelor's degree in social work (BSW) and generally a master's degree (MSW). These positions include the more common social work duties of counseling and therapeutic service provision.

Many people who go into the social work field get their first jobs after completing a bachelor's in social work (BSW) degree. With a BSW you will be prepared for work in direct service positions as a caseworker in a mental health program or county social services office. A BSW can also help you enter the corrections field as a probation, parole or corrections officer. Many child care settings also hire BSW holders to provide direct services, from providing intervention in child abuse cases to counseling in instances of misbehavior or, in a case of a learning disability, providing references for testing or other advocacy or support. A BSW can lead to positions such as case manager, providing long-term services and addressing clients' concrete needs, such as housing and medical care. But since the degree offers only limited upward mobility, most people go on to earn a master's degree.

Visit Vault at **www.vault.com** for insider company profiles, expert advice, career message boards, expert resume reviews, the Vault Job Board and more.

VAULT CAREER LIBRARY   35

Since not all colleges offer this degree at the bachelor's level, you may need to do some research to find a program or one comparable. BSWs require four years of study (as with most bachelor's programs) and can help propel you into a career in social work quickly by providing the opportunity to receive a MSW in only one year through the advanced standing program. (We will talk more about this option in the MSW section.) A BSW program is completed in the typical four years and you'll be expected to take courses related to social work specifically as well as complete a well-rounded liberal arts program. Classes may include introductory courses in psychology, sociology, human sexuality, childhood behavior/psychology and human behavior as well as some sort of research methods course. This is in addition to the basics like English, history, math (yes, you'll still have to take a math class or two) and a science course.

An internship is required for this degree, as with the master's-level programs. Generally in your third and/or fourth year, you'll be required to take a seminar in social work, which is basically an internship at an organization providing direct services to clients. In some schools, you may have to find your own internship by cold-calling agencies to see if there are any opportunities. Other schools have developed relationships with agencies and can prearrange placements for students. You will be graded, usually on a pass/fail scale, on your understanding of social work theory and practice methods, and your ability to provide competent services. You will be supervised and evaluated by someone at the organization as well as your faculty advisor on campus.

How to choose a BSW

Deciding on a BSW program is much like picking a college for any degree. You should consider cost, location, school atmosphere and rankings. Depending on what school you attend, a BSW program can cost anywhere from $15,000 to $100,000, and realistically, you will earn in the upper-20K to mid-30K range upon graduation. Bachelor's degrees in closely related fields such as sociology, psychology can lead to similar jobs, but they cannot propel you into an advanced standing MSW degree. When choosing a BSW program, keep in mind that it must be accredited by the Counsel on Social Work Education (CSWE), the regulatory body of social work education programs, in order for your credits to be applied towards a Master's degree program.

The BSW degree is a smart avenue to pursue if you are really interested in social work. It will shave at least one year of study off of your master's program, which will in turn save you money. For those who may want to complete the two-year MSW anyway (even though you have a BSW), you may be able to take more elective courses, since you will likely be able to waive many of the first-year foundation courses the MSW requires. This will give you more exposure to different course topics.

If you cannot find a BSW program or are already enrolled in another undergraduate program but want to gain exposure to social work, try registering for a social work course at your college or at a local graduate school. A complete list of accredited BSW and MSW schools is located in the appendix.

Master's Degree

Master's-level social workers, or MSWs, have completed specialized study with a particular population, social condition or area of practice within the social work field. MSWs provide more specialized services, like substance use counseling and school social work, and intensive therapy, and can become program administrators and supervise staff, including other social workers.

Your grades are only part of what will make you an attractive candidate for an MSW program. Your experience in areas related to social work will also count towards your entrance. Schools want well-rounded candidates who will prove to be assets in the field, so it's important to come to the table with as much experience as possible.

A master's degree in social work (MSW) is generally the minimum required degree for positions involving clinical, supervisory, research or administrative duties. If you are interested in private practice, you will also need to have a master's degree. There are three common types of MSW programs; two-year, reduced residency and advanced standing. Some schools offer more options, such as 16-month programs, in which students complete the degree in four consecutive semesters including the summer, and the extended program that allows students to take up to four years to complete their degree. Because of the hectic lifestyle of many social workers, and for those looking to change careers, these flexible options are important.

Coursework

Per the CSWE, most programs require students to complete courses in human behavior and the social environment, social welfare policy, research, social

Visit Vault at **www.vault.com** for insider company profiles, expert advice,
career message boards, expert resume reviews, the Vault Job Board and more.

VAULT CAREER LIBRARY   **37**

work practice, and an internship or field practicum. Curriculums emphasize social and economic justice, particularly for populations at risk; practice with ethnically, racially and economically diverse populations; and the evaluation of practice outcomes, to find out if what you are doing is making any difference. Although some social work schools only offer a clinical or generalist curriculum, others offer the option of more specialized study with specific populations or settings.

How to choose the right program

Choosing the right MSW program is essential in terms of the type of work you want to do and where you want to do it. Name recognition is one factor. A Columbia graduate can use the name both nationally and internationally, whereas as a smaller, rural and lesser-known school might leave employers with less of a sense of your skill level if you look for work outside of that community. But most schools have reputations in their own communities for what they do really well, and this can fluctuate. In the recent past, New York City schools were each perceived to have a different specialty; people who wanted to be managers went to Columbia, family therapists to Fordham University, community organizers to Hunter, and general therapists to NYU. Although this is only nomenclature, reputations do mean something to those who are looking to hire.

There are many social work schools that still require a GRE score, but some schools have abandoned this practice with the mind that standardized testing isn't really helpful in projecting success in a social work program. Again, cost and location are essential in deciding on what school to attend. A school in a major city with a diverse population may offer you more flexibility in terms of where and what you can practice. If you do choose to attend a smaller school in a more remote community but you do ultimately have dreams of leaving, take into account the caliber of the faculty, including their current and past research projects, their length of time in the field, particular areas of practice and availability to students outside of class.

Getting the Right Experience

Before you even begin applying to programs, getting some social work experience is key. If you did not complete a BSW, in your junior or senior year try taking a position (either paid or volunteer) at a local homeless shelter, soup kitchen or other service-oriented place. Working weekends will likely give you great exposure to the realities of the job (e.g. client behavior), because generally there are fewer staffers on shift and clients may be more "relaxed." You'll be providing an extra hand to the full-time workers by helping prepare meals, monitoring the front door, keeping the common spaces clean and engaging clients through conversation or board or card games.

A typical charge: Nancy

Nancy was in her late 60s, lived in upstate New York, and had suffered from schizophrenia for most of her life. She grew up locally, so she had family who visited her occasionally. Nancy would wake up around 5 a.m. and walk around the corner to have breakfast at a local diner. She would return around 9, just in time to argue with staff about taking her medications. She would then take a nap and wake up around lunchtime. After lunch, she might ask to be taken for a drive, maybe to look at local churches and visit the town in which she grew up. In the summer, staff might take her to the local fair and out for ice cream.

An experience like this can help a candidate make an informed choice about the type of social work she might want to practice, as well as making her more attractive to graduate schools. In this particular instance, familiarity with the less pleasant behaviors of people with schizophrenia, including name-calling, arguing and occasional violent outbursts can help a candidate decide whether she can do this on a daily basis. It will also give her, and prospective schools, insight into her conflict resolution, patience and reasoning skills.

Making the Right Choice

The decision to attend graduate school should be taken as seriously as the undergraduate process. You should attend open houses, sit in on classes, talk to admissions people and students, and just walk around campus to see what kind of vibe you get. If you rely only on location and reputation without ever interacting with a live person or physically visiting the school, you could be in for a huge surprise.

Contact

Contact all of the schools in your desired location and order application materials. Review these materials scrupulously, because your future livelihood will depend on it! Think about all of the research you put into your last big purchase-car, house, washing machine, iPod, computer-and multiply that by 10.

Skim the fat

Make a list of the most important attributes a program/school must have for you to be satisfied there. This list could include type of program, flexibility in scheduling, ranking, class size, job attainment percentages, location of the school, cost and diversity of the student body. Begin cutting your list here, if schools have less than half of the above attributes you're looking for.

Information sessions

If you can, schedule a time to attend an information session or graduate fair for schools you're interested in. At these events, current students, alumni, faculty and staff are available to discuss the overall program, special features, and answer questions you may have. Admissions officers generally take names and phone numbers of attendees, and can follow up on specific questions you have, or have a current student contact you for a more in-depth conversation about the school. Information sessions generally include a tour of the school and a chance to meet key people like the dean and director of admissions-you may want to have some intelligent questions ready!

On campus

Another way to get a feel for a school is to sit in on a class to gauge student-faculty interaction, teaching methods and the level of material being taught. Usually, you'll be encouraged by the professor to interact with the class, but not put on the spot if you don't voluntarily engage. What you're really looking for here is whether you're able to handle the level of information being taught and if it's interesting enough to keep you there for two years.

Schedule a one-on-one interview with the school to get the answers to questions specific to your situation. This will also give the admissions team a chance to check you out, so come dressed appropriately and ready to answer as well as ask questions.

The application

Even though you may have chosen the right school for you, it might not choose to admit you. With estimates that reach into the 2.6 million range for the number of applicants to graduate programs by 2015, you need to stand out in an increasingly large crowd.

Most graduate applications have three main components: the application and transcripts, personal reference and personal statement. Most schools will not begin processing your application until all pieces are received. Your references should be able to attest to your ability to comprehend social work theories, ability to work with diverse populations and overall predict your success in a social work program. References can include professors that you have made a particular connection with or in whose course you have done exceptionally well. Work, internship and volunteer supervisors are appropriate. Family friends (especially social workers) who know your professional goals may also be good references.

Essays or personal statements may ask you to answer either specific questions the school is interested in knowing about you or general ones around your interest/understanding of social work. Since you won't be present when the admissions committee reviews your application, it's important that your essay speak for you. It needs to convey your genuine interest in the field and the school. Beyond academics, social work schools want to know that you'll be a professional asset to the field.

When writing an essay, if the question is "why you are choosing social work" and the answer is a personal tragedy, be very brief about the actual incident and talk more about the techniques that the person who helped you, if applicable, used to make you feel empowered or able to go on. Or you may want to talk about what you wished were offered to you and why you think it was important. The best option if you are talking from personal experience is to globalize the issue with regard to others in similar situations, either as a good thing about the profession or as something that is missing that you feel you can enhance.

In terms of GPAs, each school has its own criteria for entrance, and generally at least a 3.0 is necessary. Don't get discouraged if this is not the case for you, though; there may be things you can do to help increase your chances of being accepted. Some schools may require that you retake a course and earn a better grade while enrolled in a master's program; others may grant you entrance on the condition that you achieve at least a 3.0 for your first semester; and still some may decide that your experience weighs more heavily than your grades. This last scenario may be especially true for people who have been out of school for a while but have been working in the social work field.

Visit Vault at **www.vault.com** for insider company profiles, expert advice, career message boards, expert resume reviews, the Vault Job Board and more.

VAULT CAREER LIBRARY   **41**

All schools of social work are regulated by the CSWE, so there will be similarities across the board. These include a first-year foundations course that builds on the liberal arts base most receive as undergrads, while also introducing students to the pertinent areas of social work such as ethics, concerns, values and approaches. Courses at this level include human behavior and the social environment (HBSE), policy, research methods and a general introduction to social work practice.

Courses of Study

Below is a brief description of popular courses of study in most MSW programs.

Clinical practice

Clinical practice prepares students to work with groups, individuals and/or communities, providing mental health services for the prevention, diagnosis and treatment of mental, behavioral and emotional disorders. The overall goal for this field of practice is to enhance and maintain patients' physical, psychological and social function. Course work includes particular attention to assessment of client needs, crisis intervention and evaluation of the mental functioning of clients. Risk and resiliency theories and clinical issues related to specific client populations are emphasized to make students aware of the particular issues of those they serve. You may take a course in contemporary social problems that highlights emerging ills like violence, HIV/AIDS and homelessness from a historical perspective and offers strategies to engage and assist those within these groups. People who choose this method are generally interested in pursuing a therapeutic or counseling position, either providing one-on-one counseling, facilitating support groups or developing a private practice.

Social administration/management

This track teaches the knowledge, skills and values necessary to direct or manage social service programs, such as community mental health programs. The course work centers on programs and services planning, evaluation of the services' effectiveness, financial management, staff development and training, human resource management and management information systems, such as databases of client demographics and human resources information. This orientation is likely to attract people who want to become program coordinators or administrators in public or private agencies, work in human resources or provide technical assistance/consulting services to those seeking to start new programs or reevaluate existing ones for effectiveness.

Research

This track emphasizes the understanding, design and methodology of social research, which mostly involves trying to cure social ills. Course work includes designing a research project from hypothesis to discussion and evaluation. If you are interested in conducting research yourself or assisting on someone else's project, this method is for you. Research-oriented social workers help with the development of evidence-based interventions or standardized best practices for working with specific populations and social problems, such as the use of legal needle exchanges in reducing HIV transmission among intravenous drug users. These interventions, if found credible and feasible are then adopted by organizations and held as the standard or basis for treatment within that population or issue.

Similar to for-profits like Merrill Lynch or Google, many nonprofit organizations aim to become "experts" or the final authority on the populations they serve. Organizations like the Gay Men's Health Crisis (GMHC) and the American Cancer Society (ACS) want their name to come to mind whenever an issue related to their particular niche, whether that's domestic violence, HIV/AIDS or child abuse, is raised. Once seen as the authority, these organizations are then able to inform the policies that will ultimately benefit their client populations. Researchers also help agencies evaluate their services to find areas for improvement.

Clinical/administrative track

This is a unique model that bridges the gap between clinical practice and administration. Students complete a generalist clinical social work program, including a general overview of working with different populations as well as taking courses in program development and design. This track can provide an excellent foundation for work with various populations, while also providing a solid understanding of the fiscal and programmatic perimeters all social workers contend with. Those who are torn between clinical practice and the management track might consider this option, since it fosters competency in direct services with clients as well as management of programs that provides those services.

Policy

These students learn the knowledge, values and skills to understand and delineate policy issues from a social work perspective. You may be asked to collect and analyze data to develop policy options, prepare testimony and present your recommendations to community boards or legislators. You may also be the policy analyst for a large governmental agency and therefore the spokesperson on issues related to social policy.

Community organizing

These majors learn the skills necessary to mobilize communities to make changes to enhance their quality of life. Mobilizing resources (money, politicians, community leaders, police, etc.) is also emphasized in this track, because without resources, no change is sustainable. Students write proposals/grants, evaluate programs slated to change or be eliminated, conduct outreach to provide vital information to community members and advocate with local and federal legislators.

International social work

This track offers students who want to make a change on a global level the foundation to do so. Students are prepared to work abroad on issues like disease, war and famine, with agencies such at the World Health Organization, UNICEF and AIDS service organizations. Internships in this field could include traveling abroad to conduct research or provide direct services. Visit isw.org for more information and to locate accredited programs.

Group Work

In a group work program, students learn the techniques to create, conduct and manage effective therapeutic groups. You will learn the stages of group formation, how to use groups in different settings and with particular populations. Techniques for engaging group participants and prescreening potential members are also taught. Groups have proven successful in the treatment of many populations, including children, families, the mentally ill and in vocational settings. Additionally, insurance companies have been leaning positively toward group work interventions, as they are more cost efficient.

Check Out Receipt

Harold Washington Library Center

Tuesday, August 8, 2023 3:32:29 PM

Item: R0412768202
Title: Vault career guide to social work
Due: 8/29/2023

Total items: 1

Thank you.

388

Postgraduate Programs

Two-year

The most common MSW program is two years. Within this timeframe, you are expected to learn advanced knowledge of social work theories and practice, and complete an internship at two different placements. Typically, students earn 60 credits and 1,200 field instruction hours, approximately three days a week, seven hours a day. A typical schedule includes two days of in-class learning and three days of internship. In the first year, you might take a three-hour practice and theory course, which will lay the foundation of what is expected of you in the field, along with courses in research, policy and human behavior. Most of these courses are standards in all MSW programs. In your second year, you'll be able to take more specialized courses in your field of interest.

Advanced standing

The advanced standing program is tied to the BSW degree. This program recognizes that at the end of a BSW program you are basically a first-year master's student, so the program is only one year. It is an intense year though, as you have to pick your population and setting upon entrance and only have one 600-hour field placement. If you have planned well, obtaining a BSW and then an MSW is a smart way to go. You save a whole year of tuition on the master's program, which, depending on where you go, could be worth upwards of $30,000. That will make your new salary look that much better!

Flexible, extended and reduced residency

Those who need to work while in school, caring for family or having otherwise unpredictable lives may want to look into some of the flexible schooling options, such as extended programs and one-year-residency or reduced residency programs. In the extended program, you have about four years to complete your degree from your start date, and the option of part-time study. This could be helpful if you have a job or family needs that are particularly overwhelming at certain times of the year. But take note-some courses are only offered at specific times during the academic year. Career changers might consider this option as well, as it allows you to check out the program before committing to the profession (although you will have to pay the regular course tuition).

Visit Vault at **www.vault.com** for insider company profiles, expert advice, career message boards, expert resume reviews, the Vault Job Board and more.

VAULT CAREER LIBRARY   **45**

Reduced residency and one-year-residency (OYR) programs are geared toward those working in the human services field already. In fact, some programs require that you be employed in the field for at least two years at the time of your application. Usually, in this three-year program, you attend foundation classes your first year, complete an internship at your place of employment your second year and then return for classes in your third year. One caveat is that this program usually requires that your place of employment agree to offer you an internship placement as a condition of your application. This becomes tricky because you may be required to change at least 50 percent of your job functions and client population (meaning that you might not be able to perform your regular work duties and might need to physically change your department or work site), and depending on the size of organization you work for, this may not be possible.

Dual-degree programs

Many universities offer dual degrees, which allow you to obtain your MSW in conjunction with another degree like law, public health, theology and teaching. In general these programs require meeting the entrance requirements for both programs, increased tuition and the addition of one or two years to complete both degrees. Also, there may be a requirement for additional internships based on which program you choose. If you are interested in a dual degree, you may need to declare that at the beginning of your master's program so that your primary program can be adjusted to compensate for the additional degree requirements.

Doctoral degree

In social work, the doctoral degree is usually called either a DSW or a PhD. Though DSW stands for "Doctorate in Social Work" and PhD stands for "Doctorate in Philosophy," there is no difference in the degrees; some schools just use one term over the other. The doctoral degree is the last rung of the social work educational hierarchy. Those who pursue the PhD are generally interested in research, being published as an authority on a particular subject or teaching at the college level, which may take them out of direct service work completely. PhDs who stay in academia work in schools or departments of social work where research, publication and teaching become their primary focus. To stay connected with populations of interest, they can also provide intensive long-term direct counseling services to individuals and groups as private practitioners and within agencies, while continuing to teach or research.

Doctoral degrees may take between two and four years to complete and much of the course work in these programs emphasizes qualitative and quantitative analysis methods. Like all doctoral degrees, these degrees also require students to complete dissertations, which are usually extensive research projects that take more than a year to complete. Those who earn doctoral degrees are typically seasoned professionals, but one student cited her inability to find a job in her chosen field of children services as the reason she went back to earn her PhD within one-year of graduating with her MSW.

Internships

At the heart of any social work program is the internship. This is where you are able to put the entire classroom learning into practice.

Field learning experience

Most programs require that 1200 hours of internship be completed prior to your graduation from a master's program. (For advanced standing programs, the requirement is only half the hours.) In most programs, the school, not the student, chooses the placement for the first year, except in advanced standing programs. In the second year, the student chooses a placement based on his or her area of interest or population of interest. The theory behind this practice is to ensure that students gain well-rounded experience with diverse populations and practice settings, as opposed to only working with one population or issue.

Placements often mirror employment options, meaning that wherever a social worker can be hired, a student can intern. Settings include hospitals, government agencies, community programs and substance use clinics. A student might be placed in a nursing home, in charge of planning the recreational and health awareness activities for the residents. In a mental health clinic, a student might provide therapy to crime victims. Or in a school, one might work with teens to avoid abusive relationships or deal with difficult home lives.

Your field experience will also coincide with work you are doing in the classroom, providing the subjects for papers, analysis and research projects, as well as examples of client needs and disorders you will study. This experience should be taken extremely seriously; think of your internship as a really long job interview without the pressure. As an intern, you can make mistakes and they will be deemed "learning moments" rather than "reasons

Visit Vault at **www.vault.com** for insider company profiles, expert advice, career message boards, expert resume reviews, the Vault Job Board and more.

V/\ULT CAREER LIBRARY   **47**

for termination." You will interact with others in the field and learn from their experiences.

A Sample Internship

Janice, a MSW candidate in the clinical/administrative track, interned three days a week at a psychiatric hospital in Queens, N.Y., as an intensive case manager. Her clients were all diagnosed with serious and persistent mental illness (SPMI), such as schizophrenia, bipolar disorder and major depression. Many of them also had co-occurring substance abuse issues, such as alcohol, crack or marijuana dependency. A typical client was a 33-year-old Hispanic male, living in his own apartment or in a home with family, who had been diagnosed for two years or more with mental illness. Janice's duties included making weekly home visits to all clients to evaluate their ability to live on their own, ascertain that they were taking their medications, and provide counseling to help them manage daily tasks.

One client, Jason, a 21-year-old African-American male, had been diagnosed with major depression since he was an adolescent. He grew up in an abusive home where his mother provided minimal supervision or nurturing. As a teenager, he was involved with the "goth" culture and dressed all in black, wore spiked jewelry and had multiple piercings in his face and ears. Approximately halfway through the year, Janice began to wonder if Jason had been correctly diagnosed. What she noticed was that Jason would change his demeanor and feelings based on the person he was talking to. Janice had an upbeat personality, whereas her supervisor was more serious and sullen. When Janice and her supervisor visited Jason together, Jason would take on the personality features of the supervisor, talking in a low tone and expressing feelings of ambivalence and a flat affect. But when Janice visited alone, his demeanor was more "normal," he seemed less depressed and talked about his future plans.

Janice discussed her observations with her supervisor and he suggested they monitor Jason for one month to see if the pattern held. It did. The next step was to approach Jason's psychiatrist and request that he be reevaluated for a personality disorder rather than major depression. In the end, Jason's diagnosis was changed to reflect a personality disorder and his treatment was altered to match. As a result, Jason began to show positive signs of treatment, including becoming more active, and even began dating.

What happened in this situation wasn't that Janice's supervisor was negligent; it was that her fresh pair of eyes saw something different then his did. This kind of experience is what can make internships worthwhile; students walk into already existing programs with enrolled clients and not only have a chance to learn but also to enhance what is already there.

It is not uncommon, when working with the same client for a long time, to begin to see them only through the lens of their diagnosis instead of as a person with a dynamic personality. In social work, it is always important to remember to treat whole people, not just a diagnosis.

Licensure

According to the Association of Social Work Boards (ASWB), the purpose of licensing and certification in social work is to assist the public through identification of standards for the safe professional practice of social work. Currently, all 50 states have some form of licensure or registration for social work practice. Since different states have different requirements, you should check with your state's office of professions or contact ASWB or NASW for information about your state's requirements. Generally, there are four types of licensure for social workers that may be legally regulated:

Bachelor's: Baccalaureate social work degree upon graduation;

Master's: Master's degree in social work (MSW) with no post-degree experience;

Advanced Generalist: MSW with two years of post-master's supervised experience;

Clinical: MSW with two years of post-master's direct clinical social work experience.

In most states, licensure requires a standardized test with a passing score, an application, and may also require the completion of a course in child abuse and neglect. There are fees (about $175) associated with the test that may vary by state, as well as preliminary requirements, such as length of time in the field, a required number of hours spent in clinical supervision with a licensed social worker, and work with a specific population or practice type. Supervision by a licensed social worker may be done at your place of employment, if your boss is licensed, or you may seek what is termed

Visit Vault at **www.vault.com** for insider company profiles, expert advice, career message boards, expert resume reviews, the Vault Job Board and more.

V/\ULT CAREER LIBRARY   **49**

"outside supervision" where you hire a licensed social worker on a fee basis to supervise you, and they in turn certify that you attended for the requisite number of hours. Social workers who maintain private practices or who have been in the field for a number of years are likely to offer this type of service for varying fees.

Paying for Your Education

From the bachelor's level through to the PhD, the costs of a social work education can be anywhere from $15,000 to over $100,000 when all is said and done, so it is wise to do your homework about ways to offset the cost. Most schools offer some type of financial aid to students in the form of grants, loans or scholarships, and most students are eligible for federal loans for undergraduate and graduate programs, but these may not cover all of the costs. You may find it necessary to take out the maximum amount of federal loans, utilize work study and still need to find private monies from scholarships to cover all of your tuition and living expenses.

Most schools have a directory of available scholarship opportunities for students in their financial aid offices. Generally, above B grades are required for these scholarships, so application may have to wait until after your first year. There are some scholarships and grants that are offered based on gender, age, ethnic background or life circumstance. Other scholarships will offer loan reimbursement of $10,000 for funds you have already taken out to pay for your education. Visit your prospective school's web site or call its financial aid office for information on scholarship, endowment and grant programs for which you may be eligible. See the appendix for a selected list of financial aid resources.

The Job Search

CHAPTER 5

Starting a New Search

The most important part of looking for a job starts before you even open a newspaper, click onto a web site or ask a friend for a referral. Here are some questions to ask yourself as you begin your job search:

- **What type of social work can I/do I want to do?** Is it therapy or counseling, or does assessment and referral sound more like the work you want to do? How about administrative work? Will you be happy not having much client contact while directing a program? Do you have enough experience or credentialing to do the type of social work you want? This is a good time to review any volunteer or internship experience you may have. What skills did you learn in these positions that you think could be helpful in a social work career?

- **What type of people do I want to work with?** Would you prefer to work with children, adults, adolescents, families, the elderly, substance users, mentally ill people or immigrants?

- **What type of setting do I want to work in?** Do you thrive in a 9-to-5 position that carries minimal paperwork or stress? Or does the fast pace of a hospital or school sound better? How about the physical environment of your workspace, cubicle vs. office with a door? Do you want your office on the same floor that clients congregate on or on a different one? Nonprofit or corporate environment?

- **Are there positions where I live or will I have to commute?** In major metropolitan areas, social work positions abound, but in less populated regions that may not be the case. Are you willing to travel into a city or move altogether in order to find a job?

There are several different ways to go about looking for employment. Web sites, newspapers, networking and career services offices are the most useful options. And remember that even though your first position may not be your dream job, it is important that you start off on the right foot by making the right decision based on your skills, desires and future goals.

Sample Job Search

Before even graduating from her MSW program, Krystal was nervous about finding a job in New York City. Not sure if she would stay in the city or move back home to upstate New York, she began job searching the first semester of her last year. Between frequent visits to her school's career services office to check on job prospects in NYC and checking the web site of her hometown, Krystal found many opportunities. Around December, she attended an open house event hosted by a nonprofit located near her internship. This proactive approach helped her land a job before she even graduated. After going through three interviews, she was offered a position in February, as the coordinator of a program that helped people with HIV find adequate housing. The position would wait until her May graduation.

After about a year and a half, Krystal felt she wanted to do more therapeutic work and increase her salary. She found her second job, as a program manager of a supportive counseling program, through a social work web site and was hired by an alumnus of her graduate school. This position would allow her to use her management skills, but also provide therapy to mentally ill clients. Within a year, this program shut down due to withdrawal of state funding.

Krystal's current position is in the training and staff development department of a large nonprofit. This job relies on the training skills she gained during her second-year student internship, as Krystal uses her own experiences and proficiency in research and curriculum development to teach other staff how to effectively engage and assist agency clients.

Where to look

In some cases, large web sites that carry vast job listings from mostly corporate employers are not as helpful in locating a social work position if you are not in a major metropolitan area like Los Angeles, New York or Boston; more employment agencies post on these sites than actual employers. In addition, these sites may not even list social work as a specific category; you'll have to search under various headings, like health services, mental health, social services, support services or nonprofits. You also may not be able to search by degree (BSW, MSW, PhD).

A better idea is web sites dedicated specifically to social work or human service employers, such as SocialService.com, NASW and idealist.org. These sites allow you to search and sort jobs based on your educational level, geographic location, and some even by desired salary. Some allow you to set e-mail alerts based on specific criteria you select, and when a position matching your criteria is posted it is automatically e-mailed to you.

Traditional searches in newspapers can be fruitful if you know where and when to look. For instance, The New York Times is a great resource on Sundays, but other days it is mediocre for social work positions. And take heed: some positions may not be listed under social work; you may need to look under human services, in the health/medical health section or under headings such as recreational counselor, rehabilitation specialist, counselor or other specific job titles to find what you are looking for.

University career services are also a good place to begin your job search. These offices should be knowledgeable about employment trends, offer coaching on resume writing, interviewing and negotiating skills, and they also post open positions, open houses and calls for resumes for the general student body. Some coordinate networking events that allow employers, alumni and students to mingle so students can learn about opportunities and employers can gain a sense of students' skills. These events can be particularly helpful to students who pursue nontraditional social work paths such as international work or policy social work, since the bulk of social work opportunities involve direct client work.

Networking Tips

- **Have business cards.** You can order customized cards online; these help employers remember who they met.

- **Be prepared with a resume, but don't force it on an employer.** Most of these events are mixers which allow for mingling and chatting. If you have done a good job at advertising yourself, skills and interests, an employer will ask for your resume.

- **Dress professionally.** Don't assume that because it is an after-hours mixer for social workers that employers aren't interested in traditional attire.

- **Do your homework.** Having some interesting things to say about the employers in the room based on their past work will give you a conversational edge.

Visit Vault at **www.vault.com** for insider company profiles, expert advice, career message boards, expert resume reviews, the Vault Job Board and more.

VAULT CAREER LIBRARY

53

• **Don't be shy.** No one is going to come to you; if you want a job you have to go out there and get it!

If you are interested in a particular area of social work, try doing a general search (Google it) on the Internet to find employers; this may give you a sense of what qualifications are necessary for this type of work. It's a good idea to think about doing this prior to beginning or completing you social work education, so you can tailor your course work or internship accordingly.

Newbies

Just finished a BSW or MSW program and don't have a lot of work experience? You are a newbie. Your challenge is to get employers interested in your new skills and fresh energy over more experienced workers. To do this, you want to present yourself as proficient in the social work profession-familiar with its terminology, knowledgeable of current trends and future advancements, and committed to the profession. Adequate preparation is the key. In your resume, make sure you describe the skills you needed to perform your job duties; don't just list your responsibilities.

Consider all of your jobs as experience. From working at the mall to camp counselor at summer sleep away camp to volunteering at the children's ward at the local hospital, all of these experiences have defined skills that made you successful at them. Your mission is to decipher those skills and integrate them into a powerful resume and cover letter. Some skills that you may have and don't know could be:

• Observation of clients/campers/patients for safety

• Group facilitation skills

• Intervention skills/conflict management

• Ability to work as part of a team

• Record keeping

Career Changers

You have experience in a different industry and now you have found your calling in social work. How do you translate your investment banking skills to social work? You break down your job to its most fundamental parts and find the social work skill that matches it. For instance, you may be handling investment portfolios for clients: assessing their worth and investment goals, assisting them in making investment decisions and referring them to beneficial future opportunities. Assess, Assist, Refer are fundamentals of social work practice (assessing a client's needs, assisting them in setting realistic goals to meet those needs, and referring them to appropriate services for help in reaching their goal).

When applying for social work positions, be confident in your skill set, but also be modest. You may have extensive experience in your current field of work, but you haven't been a social worker before, so some modesty and exhibiting a willingness to learn is important. During interviews you will probably be asked why you are changing career fields, so explore this reason before your first interview. Be prepared with a simple but meaningful answer that speaks to both your personal goals and globally about helping others. But be careful about how personal you get; you don't want to sound like you are choosing social work because you need therapy yourself.

Visit Vault at **www.vault.com** for insider company profiles, expert advice, career message boards, expert resume reviews, the Vault Job Board and more.

VAULT CAREER LIBRARY   **55**

V∧ULT

THE MOST TRUSTED NAME IN CAREER INFORMATION

Vault guides and employer profiles have been published since 1997 and are the premier source of insider information on careers.

Each year, Vault surveys and interviews thousands of employees to give readers the inside scoop on industries and specific employers to help them get the jobs they want.

V∧ULT

Getting the Job You Want

CHAPTER 6

Resume Writing

Before you begin writing your resume, gather all pertinent information about your past employment, volunteer, internships and education. This information includes start and end dates, salary, position title, supervisor/reference contact information and a list of accomplishments, earned achievements, memberships in clubs or professional associations.

There are different styles of resumes that you can use based on your work experience. Most people use either the chronological or skills-based resume. Each has its benefits if you know when to use them.

Chronological resumes

The most common type of resume is the chronological style. Here you simply list your job title, start and end dates and use bullet points to describe your job duties. You begin with a heading that includes your name, address, phone number and other contact information. Some people like to make their heading fancy as if it were their actual letterhead, but just make sure you are using a font that is easy to read and looks mature; curly cues do not make the best impression.

Next you list your employment objective, or the position you are applying for. Be sure to change this if you are applying for multiple positions, you don't want to send the adolescent services agency a resume stating that you are looking to work with elderly homeless people. If, however, you are seeking a position in one specific area such as in a hospital or school setting, you can use a generalized heading such as "Seeking position in social work unit of large hospital." But best practice is to customize your resume for the position you are applying to.

Next you describe your work or relevant experience. In this section you describe the work you have done in short, powerful sentences. You don't need to explain every detail of your experience, just the most relevant to the position you are applying. And there is a fine line between embellishing and lying; remember that your references will be checked.

Visit Vault at **www.vault.com** for insider company profiles, expert advice, career message boards, expert resume reviews, the Vault Job Board and more.

VAULT CAREER LIBRARY   57

Next you list your education, usually including your current and most recent past degree, for instance, undergraduate and high school, or graduate and undergraduate. If you have specialized degrees you can list these here also, but only if they pertain to the position being applied for or explain a large gap in your work history.

Lastly you have the "other" category. This is where you list your community/volunteer experience, specialized training, languages, skills or accomplishments. Positions held in professional- or school-related associations/organizations can also go here. In general, if you do not have an extensive work history, this is the type of resume you should use. It provides a clear and simply stated presentation of your experience and abilities.

Sample Chronological Resume

James Thomas
258 North West Street, New York, NY 10001
212-555-9898
JT346@email.com

Employment Interests
Clinical practice in the treatment of emotional and affective disorders

Work Experience
1992-present   Private Clinical Practice
1987-1992   Program director, Alternative to Incarceration Program

Education
Columbia University School of Social Work
Doctoral degree May 2007
Concentration: Administration in nonprofits
Dissertation: Effective Supervisory Practices in Nonprofits

University of Wisconsin
Master's of Social Work 1991
Concentration: family and children's services

Skills/Accomplishments
Co-author *Use of Emotional Intelligence Testing in Human Service Agencies with Middle Level Management.* Journal of Social Work Supervision. July 2004

Member, NY Psychoanalytic Society. 1999 to present

Fluent in French and Spanish

Visit Vault at **www.vault.com** for insider company profiles, expert advice,
career message boards, expert resume reviews, the Vault Job Board and more.

VAULT CAREER LIBRARY   59

Skills-based resume

This resume uses more of a detailed style to display your skills and experience. If you are a career changer, or have received your degree after working in the field for a number of years, you probably want to use this kind of resume, as it highlights the skills you have in your current profession, making it easier for potential employers to see how these skills can be transferred to a social work position. Like the chronological resume, the skills-based resume begins with the heading of your name, address and other contact information.

The profile section is next. This takes the place of the employment objective. In this section you describe, in general, your past work experience, putting more emphasis on the skills needed to complete your responsibilities, not just your job duty.

Next is the experience/skills section. Here you break down your skills based on categories or headings.

Then you list your employment history with only title, company name, start and end dates, and city/state.

Last is your education. The reason for putting your education last is because this style is really geared toward people who have experience and skills. If you have been out of school for a number of years or have extensive experience, your education may not be as important as your skills.

Sample Skills Resume

Stephanie Carol

43 Rogers Lane, Louton, MD 12566 • (435) 786-2214 •
SCarol65@webmail.com

Profile

Licensed MSW with four years of experience providing program management, therapeutic and concrete services to populations in need including people with mental illness, HIV/AIDS, homeless, substance using, youth and families in disadvantaged neighborhoods. Astute in the coordination and delivery of training to professional staff and community members on topics related to HIV/AIDS prevention and treatment, appropriate clinical interventions and child abuse and neglect reporting procedures.

Experience/Skills

Program coordination
Proficient in all areas of program planning and development, contract compliance, fiscal responsibility and maintaining practice standards. Competent in supervision of staff from diverse backgrounds and educational achievements

Program development and technical assistance
Expert in assessing the training needs of agencies, including pre- and post-assessment testing for learning. Proficient in the design and development of training programs based on results of needs assessment tool, agency and client input

Clinical Skills
Proven crisis intervention, counseling and conflict resolution skills. Successfully coordinates care within an interdisciplinary treatment team of psychiatrists, social workers, health care providers

Visit Vault at **www.vault.com** for insider company profiles, expert advice,
career message boards, expert resume reviews, the Vault Job Board and more.

VAULT CAREER LIBRARY

61

Sample Skills Resume (continued)

Employment History

5/2003-1/2005
Program coordinator, Housing Placement program
Homeless Organization, New York, NY

9/2002-5/2003
Social work intern
Training Institute, New York, NY

Education

Columbia University School of Social Work, New York, NY
Master of Science in Social Work, May 2003
Method: Advanced Generalist Practice and Programming
Field of Practice: Contemporary Social Problems
LMSW earned 5/2003

Resume tips

- Use only one font on your resume (excluding heading). Too many will make it look comical and will not be pleasing to the eye. Times New Roman, Arial or Courier New are your best bets.

- Make sure you are using at least 11-point font-employers are not into squinting.

- No more than two pages, but if you go over one page be sure that you have enough skills/experience to fill up both pages.

- Don't send supplemental material (degree, license, military discharge, etc.) with your resume unless it is specifically asked for.

- When applying for positions, follow the instructions exactly as the employer requests. If they only want faxes, don't e-mail your resume.

- Use powerful, descriptive words that convey ability, not just responsibility. Stay away from "able to" and "responsible for"; these words leave readers with too many questions. "Able to" means that you can do something, but have/did you do it? "Responsible for" only tells what your duty was, not what you actually did. Instead, words like "provided," "competent in" or "proficient in," "developed," "coordinated," "implemented," and "created" are better choices.

- Have friends and family look at your resume and give you constructive feedback on its five-second presentation. Some employers are more likely to read a resume based on how visually appealing it is in the first five seconds.

- Your spacing should be even (use tabs or columns), with clear sentences and sections that are easily defined.

Cover Letters

Your cover letter is just as important as your resume, as it is the employer's first introduction to you. A strong cover letter will make an employer want to read your resume. A cover letter with grammatical errors, poor word choices or from a cookie-cutter format will do just the opposite. Cover letters should convey your interest in the position, the exact position you are applying for, how you heard of the position, your qualifications, briefly mention your past experience and request an interview. You should use the same heading, or one very similar to that used on your resume, and format the cover letter using at least three paragraphs without any indentations.

Visit Vault at **www.vault.com** for insider company profiles, expert advice, career message boards, expert resume reviews, the Vault Job Board and more.

V**Λ**ULT CAREER LIBRARY   **63**

Sample Cover Letter

Stephanie Carol
43 Rogers Lane, Louton MD 12566
(435) 786-2214
Scarol65@webmail.com

June 19, 2002

Dear Mr. Parkinson,

Please accept this letter and attached resume in application for the Health Educator position listed on SocialService.com. I am a licensed social worker (LMSW) with five years of counseling experience: experience in program coordination, staff supervision and training/technical assistance. I am interested in this position as it combines my skills/knowledge in program coordination and development, counseling and training provision.

As noted in my resume, I have experience coordinating programs serving disadvantaged populations such as homeless, HIV/AIDS, mentally ill and substance users. This experience includes work with individuals, families and groups with the goal of behavior change/modification and risk reduction.

Thank you for your time in considering my application. I can be reached at the phone number or e-mail address above to discuss my interest and qualifications further.

All best,

Stephanie Carol

Cover letter tips

- Don't forget to mention how you heard of the position. This helps recruiters better target potential employees.

- PROOFREAD! Make sure you are using all words correctly and that you have no spelling mistakes (don't always rely on spell check).

- KISS-keep your cover letter simple. Too much will leave the reader too tired to read your resume. Think of it as an appetizer.

- Make sure to include any job reference numbers in the first paragraph, if directed to include them.

- Be confident but not arrogant. Telling the employer forcibly that you are an asset doesn't help, because if you were so good you wouldn't need this job. Be humble but assertive.

The Interview

The point of the interview is to bring to life the skills and abilities listed in your resume and give the employer a chance to see how your knowledge, personality and goals fit into the work environment. It is also a time for you to form impressions about your ability to work in the environment presented. Areas you should concentrate on are:

The commute and physical environment

How long is the commute-is it feasible to do every day? Office location. Will you have your own office or will you be sharing with others? Do you need to share office equipment like computers and phones?

Safety

Is the neighborhood safe if you are working late in the evening? Are there stairs or an elevator? Is security adequate/visible? How do clients gain access to the space (buzzed in by staff or able to walk in unattended)?

General atmosphere

How are clients greeted when they arrive? How were you greeted? What are people wearing-casual clothing or suits? How are people interacting with each other? Is the office busy and bustling or is it a calm environment?

Visit Vault at **www.vault.com** for insider company profiles, expert advice, career message boards, expert resume reviews, the Vault Job Board and more.

VAULT CAREER LIBRARY   **65**

These first impressions can help you form questions during the actual interview so you can be better informed about the organization's culture and make assumptions about your general happiness in the event that you are hired.

Group interviews

Some organizations, generally larger ones or those that offer comprehensive services where it's common for colleagues from different departments to work as a team, will conduct group interviews with multiple candidates to save time and resources. There may be up to five other people and a panel of three interviewers. The best way to approach these is to try to stand out for your expertise, not only your personality. Answer the questions truthfully from your experience, and avoid embellishing just to outdo the person who went before you. When in doubt, the phrase "I would defer to the organization's policy and procedures," can be helpful.

Interview tips

- Be at least 10 minutes early; any earlier and you may be interrupting the interviewer.

- Have a fresh copy of your resume and any information necessary to complete an employment application.

- Ask questions for clarification, but allow the interviewer to lead the conversation.

- Be prepared to answer specific questions about your past work/volunteer/educational experience.

- You may ask questions related to the position's duties, possibility of advancement and general organizational culture.

- Find a positive way to explain negative experiences with past employers or clients; don't badmouth past employers.

- Answer questions truthfully, but don't offer too much information.

- Try not to ask about salary until at least the second interview; if this information is not offered and you are only marginally interested in the position or are weighing it with another, it is OK to ask so you can decide if another interview is worth your and the employer's time. Be tactful if you take this route.

- Send a follow-up thank-you letter only if you are genuinely interested in the position.

Deciding on an Offer

Many first-time job-seekers think they must take the first position offered, exactly how it is offered. This isn't true. A job offer is just that; an offer. You can ask that it be altered, within reason, and if not you can decline it altogether. When asking to enhance an offer, be prepared to offer a reason as to why. Some valid reasons to ask for increased salary are: you were making significantly more money at a previous position; you have exceptional skills/training/knowledge relevant to the position you are applying for; the position requires supervision of other staff or other administrative-related duties; the job includes projects in addition to your regular job duties. Before asking for more money, be sure to weigh the benefits (vacation time, sick, health insurance coverage) of the position also. A good health insurance plan can cost hundreds of dollars a month; if your job can offer it to you for less than $50, it is certainly worth considering.

You may be weighing more than one option at a time. How to decide? First, think of your ideal position, then list the skills or experience you will need to earn that job. Now match this list to what you are being offered. Which one most closely allows you to gain, utilize or refine these skills? Then think about your lifestyle and which position will allow maintaining it or enhancing it. Lastly, imagine yourself in this position for two years. Did you smile or did your face begin to tighten up? If the latter occurred, you may need more time to make this decision. A good employer will understand this, but don't be too greedy. Asking for an extra day or two is OK, but a week is really pushing it. It may show that you are unsure of what you want and can't make critical decisions, not great traits in a potential employee.

Accepting a position is the easy part; you simply tell your future employer that you are interested in the position and would like to accept. Usually the conversation will go smoothly and you will be connected with human resources to complete the necessary paperwork. But what happens when you want to decline the offer? Simply state the opposite: "Thank you for your time, but I have decided to accept another position." There may be a period of dead air in which you will feel compelled to begin explaining your decision-don't. If they are interested in the reasons why you are declining the offer they will ask; if not, they won't. Unless you have really valid reasons that will help the agency in their future recruiting efforts, such as a cumbersome application/interviewing process that left you with more questions than answers, or the job was completely different than advertised or the salary just did not match up with the experience required, you should keep your comments to yourself. The tactful decline will benefit you in future in small communities or in various industries like the nonprofit world; you may have to

Visit Vault at **www.vault.com** for insider company profiles, expert advice, career message boards, expert resume reviews, the Vault Job Board and more.

VAULT CAREER LIBRARY

67

interact with the agency in your current position or may want to apply for a different position within that agency in the future.

Considering benefits

You know your salary, but that isn't enough. When weighing job options you have to take into account the benefits package also. Most packages include health/dental insurance, vacation, sick leave, personal days, retirement savings options and access to an employee assistance program. Although your salary may be $46,000, once you factor in all of the benefits paid by your employer, the cost of your employment could balloon to half or more of your take home salary. A good benefits package can make a lower-salary position more desirable based on your individual needs. A person with two small children may opt to take a lower-salaried position because it offers no-cost health insurance, whereas a higher-paid position might require the employee to contribute to the cost. If you are someone who enjoys time off, the difference in allotted vacation days may make one offer better than the other. Additionally, employers sometimes have supplementary benefits that include discounts at local attractions such as Broadway shows or movie theaters, gym memberships, access to trainings based on your job responsibilities and options for tuition reimbursement for related school expenses while working.

Simply because you are offered a position with a specified salary and benefits package does not mean there isn't any room to negotiate. Most employers assume there will be some bargaining that happens during the hiring process; you have to be on your A-game to make the best deal. As a first-year graduate without any experience your bargaining options may be quite limited. But you do still have options. If you can cite specific skills that may be rare or in demand in your chosen field, and guarantee to put them into action, that could be worth another $1,500 to $3,000 more per year. These skills might include proficiency in a second language that is prevalent within the client population you're serving; another degree, such as a law degree, that can help clients in navigating legal issues without having to actually hire an attorney; or experience with computer or database systems if your agency lacks an IT department or is migrating to a new system.

The same applies to benefits. You may negotiate for more time off or no-cost insurance if you can prove you are worth it. Simply making more money or having more time off at a previous job won't be enough to sway a future employer but medical needs, family obligations or making the case for your knowledge, skills and abilities may. You may need to provide evidence that your nontraditional plan would work, so be ready with some sort of proposal that clearly outlines the benefits for the agency. If you want to be able to work from home one day a week because it would reduce your childcare costs, be prepared to bottom-line it for your boss-will this change save them money by reducing the cost of electricity at your work station? Could your work be done more efficiently at home because you have a more sophisticated computer/internet system? Would the rise in childcare costs ultimately force you to quit and cause the company to spend money advertising your position, interviewing candidates and training a new person?

The bottom line in accepting, declining or negotiating an offer is that you must be honest with yourself. Be as sure as you can that you will be satisfied with this position and that it will ultimately lead you to where you want to be.

Example Decision

Recently, New York social worker Teddy was juggling three offers at one time. Each job was in a very different area of social work, and varied in salary. One position was as a supportive counselor for adults with HIV in which he would offer short-term therapy; salary was in the low $40,000s. The next position was as a trainer with a large victim services agency, providing clinical training to all staff in the agency, with a salary range in the upper $40,000s. Last was a position as a program coordinator for an after-school program with adolescents who provide outreach and education to their peers on HIV/AIDS; salary in the mid-$40,000s. With each of these offers he had to weigh three important factors: longevity of the position, commute and ability to build skills for use in his "dream job."

The position Teddy chose provided the best outcome from all three perspectives. The position he was leaving was funded by government dollars, and recently funding had been cut, meaning Teddy was essentially out of a job. Teddy didn't want this to happen again, so he looked for positions where the salary didn't derive from a government grant. The HIV counselor and after-school program coordinator positions he was offered were grant-funded, which meant that if the programs failed to meet set standards or the funder no longer provided the money to run the program, it would end, along with Teddy's job. (This is something very important to think about and certainly ask about during the interview phase. You'll want to know how long a contract has been in existence, how it has been performing and what the refunding terms are.)

Secondly, Teddy was interested in a shorter commute that would leave him more personal time, and the position he chose offered this to him as well. In the past, Teddy had commutes of up to 1.5 hours;

Visit Vault at **www.vault.com** for insider company profiles, expert advice, career message boards, expert resume reviews, the Vault Job Board and more.

VAULT CAREER LIBRARY   **69**

the new job gave him the choice or walking or taking a 15-minute train ride.

Lastly, one of Teddy's ultimate career goals is to start a consulting firm that works with nonprofits to create innovative programming for clients. To do this, he knew he would require good needs assessment, training and collaborating skills along with expertise in a certain field. The trainer position with the victim services agency offered him all of these skills. Teddy's clear awareness about his job objectives was instrumental in helping decide which position to accept.

Planning Your Career

Whether this is your first job, a new career path or you're a veteran social worker, it's critical to make the most of every position you hold. Taking learning opportunities seriously as opposed to viewing them as an extra burden outside of your regular duties can be crucial in making career moves in social work. For instance, a seasoned employee may be asked to "act as" the head of a program or department in the absence of an actual director due to resignation or illness. This might involve taking on the duties of running the program, making major decisions, budgeting, report preparation and staff supervision. Stepping up to this challenge may give those above you a different, more positive picture of your skills and abilities. The added responsibilities may mean longer hours and more complicated tasks, but you may ultimately find yourself promoted into the position instead of your supervisors hiring from outside. Additionally, you will be compensated for the added duties.

Seek out training that enhances or teaches new skills. If you know, for example, that training and staff development is where you want to be, maximize opportunities to go to trainings on topics related to presentation skills, effective writing, employee relations or curriculum development, and then reinforce what you've learned with your staff and colleagues by briefing them on the training and coaching them to use the new techniques. Eventually, you may be asked to head up a task force providing internal training to managers on agency policy and procedures because of your interest and demonstrated skills.

Finally, staying abreast of developments in the field and the population you serve, joining professional organizations, such as a local chapter of the National Association of Social Workers (NASW), School Social Worker Association of America (SSWAA) or the Association of Pediatric Oncology Social Workers (APOSW). Last but not least, making friends with other social workers can be invaluable to a successful career in social work.

ON THE JOB

Career Tracks

This chapter will discuss what social workers actually do from day to day, delving into various career tracks, such as family and children services, school social work, medical social work, mental health, substance abuse, clinical social work, government, nonprofit and other opportunities. Highlighted in each career path are the salaries, pros and cons and advancement opportunities available.

A note on salary

When considering salary, it is important to take into account the field of practice you choose, whether you'll be licensed, the number of years you are in practice and the number of years spent in the same organization. In 2002, the Practice Research Network reported a positive correlation between length of time in practice and increased salary. Full-time social workers in 1999 earned an average of $45,000 that increased to $49,000 in 2001. The highest earners worked for private, for-profit companies in which highest reported incomes hover around $70,000. The lowest salaries tended to be in sectarian nonprofits, with high earnings in the low $50,000s. Overall, those with over two years' experience saw an increase from $42,500 to $62,500; median for the same years in practice was $30,000 to $39,000.

Family and Children Services

With proper educational and experiential training, it is relatively easy to get a job in this field. In fact, most social workers have done some type of work in family and children's services in their career. To gain entry-level positions pre- or post-bachelor's program, try interning or working at a child care facility, the children's ward at a hospital or taking specialized courses in child development.

Salaries in this field range from the high $20,000s to the mid $30,000s for entry-level positions that require at least a BSW but prefer a MSW. For positions that have some supervisory duties or more intensive work with clients the range is high $30s to high $40s. Coordinators and above are high $40s to upper $60s depending on the agency you work for. Religious and government agencies tend to have higher salaries than nonprofits.

Visit Vault at **www.vault.com** for insider company profiles, expert advice, career message boards, expert resume reviews, the Vault Job Board and more.

VAULT CAREER LIBRARY   73

Opportunities for advancement in this field are profound. It is very common for social workers who begin as caseworkers in city child welfare agencies to become supervisors and eventually directors with the proper work ethic and educational background. For entry-level positions a BSW is generally required, and for supervisory positions an MSW is required with training in child development or family dynamics. NASW has two special certifications for those in this field called the Certified Children, Youth and Family Social Worker (C-CYFSW) and the Certified Advanced Children, Youth, and Family Social Worker (C-ACYFSW). These nationally recognized credentials are obtained only through NASW after the worker has completed at least one year of postgraduate employment in a child and family services setting and has been supervised by another social worker during that time. These certifications do not guarantee any additional salary compensation, but you will stand out as a professional and an expert in this field.

Family and children services: pluses and minuses

There are many challenges in this field of practice and it requires specific training and skills to understand each family. These social workers can play an important role in the lives of children and their progress towards adulthood. Of the many challenges, one of the biggest is when no help can be offered except for splitting the family for the welfare of the abused or neglected member. At these times, it is important to look at the silver lining, that at least the member will no longer be harmed and hopefully the perpetrator is getting help.

School Social Work

Employment of school social workers is expected to grow as efforts expand to respond to rising student enrollments at all grade levels. In addition, there's been a continued emphasis on integrating children with disabilities into the mainstream school population, so school social workers are increasingly needed in that capacity. But the availability of federal, state and local funding will be a major factor in determining the actual job growth in schools. The median income of social workers in elementary and secondary school settings was $44,300 in 2004.

Advancement in this field can be minimal, as there is not much hierarchy within schools for social workers. Mobility within this setting generally requires movement from one school district to another for increased salary, benefits or a different student population. In most schools, social workers report directly to the principal for supervision, guidance and issues related to the work, or there may be a designated supervising social worker in the school district who handles these matters.

To break into this type of work, volunteering or being a teacher's aide at the school or district you are interested in can be helpful. This will allow you to gain insight into the school's culture, students' behavior and needs, and allow the principal to see your work firsthand. Some large municipal school districts hire from a list similar to civil service lists, while smaller districts usually rely on referrals from existing staff. Either way, familiarity with the school and the district is beneficial to gaining employment there.

School social work: pluses and minuses

School social work is well suited to someone who can handle an unpredictable day, since in schools with upwards of 3,000 students you never know when someone will walk in your door or what their issue will be. It should go without saying, but you must be fond of children in this line of work, as they will be your primary clients. The satisfaction from helping a student or family sort out a problem and watching the success of the solution can also be an immeasurable plus in this field. And, of course, you'll get summers off!

There are also disadvantages. For instance, in inner-city schools where space is at a premium, you may find yourself without a regular office within the school you are assigned. Having an office off site and needing to travel to the school during the day to see students or for after-school programming is not uncommon, and may add extra stress to this position. Additionally, since there typically tends to be only one social worker assigned per school, the lack of a colleague with whom one can discuss issues is a common complaint among social workers in this field.

Medical Social Work

In home health care settings, such as a visiting nurse service, which provide services at patients; homes, a medical social worker may be assigned to conduct home visits to patients who have an illness so severe that it restricts their mobility. During these visits, the social worker will assess the patients' adherence to their medication and diet regiment, evaluate their ability to continue living independently, talk with the patients about any reactions they may be having to the medication, and discuss how medications and the

Visit Vault at **www.vault.com** for insider company profiles, expert advice, career message boards, expert resume reviews, the Vault Job Board and more.

VAULT CAREER LIBRARY   **75**

disease are impacting their quality of life in general. These reports are usually submitted to the patients' primary care physicians with any recommendations for treatment change, and may be discussed with patients at a later medical appointment. For the most part, the goal of these visiting services is to assist people in maintaining their independence.

At hospitals with large social work departments, which can deploy social workers to various departments, advancement to department director or unit supervisor is an option. Other titles include senior social worker or clinical director, which usually carry with them responsibilities of staff supervision, staff scheduling and a patient caseload. Paperwork is also an integral part of these positions. Hospitals are very keen on tracking every minute spent with patients either for billing purposes or so there is a paper trail of care to limit liability in case of a lawsuit. Hospital social workers need to be organized enough to stay on top of this paperwork (case notes, discharge summaries, treatment recommendations, billing forms) as well as have a viable list of resources patients may access upon their return home (therapists/social workers, in-home health aides, grocery delivery services, transportation services like Access-A-Ride) in order to be effective in this position.

As a medical social worker, you will be expected to be familiar with medical terminology, disease progression and other areas particular to the setting in which you're working. Reading medical journals, such as the Journal of the American Medical Association (JAMA) or the medical social work journal published by the National Association of Social Workers (NASW), are helpful for keeping abreast of medical trends and learning about what others in the field are doing.

In 2004, the average annual salary for a medical social worker at a general medical or surgical hospital was $44,920. Within home health care settings the median was $42,710; within nursing care facilities the salary was $35,680.

Medical social work: pluses and minuses

The day of a medical social worker is unpredictable and requires a personality that can handle multiple tasks, problems and people in a calm and conscientious manner. You also need to be able to stick to your boundaries, as not every patient will get better and there will always be another patient waiting for you. So you cannot become overly involved in any one case.

If you are a person who does not like to drive or travel on public transport for most of the workday, medical social work may not be for you. You may spend upwards of four days a week visiting clients and have one administrative day to complete the necessary paperwork for that week. Organization is key. As you will probably be carrying resources, client files and other important materials with you and seeing multiple clients in one day who may live on opposite ends of the city, you'll need to find relevant documents quickly, take effective notes during visits and plan your time so that you are not late to the next visit because you allowed the first one to go over the allotted time. At the same time, many social workers in this line of work find fulfillment in these home visits. Sadly, they may be the only person who visits the patient with any regularity, providing a break for a client from the monotony of being homebound.

Because of the hierarchy generally found in the medical field (where doctors are considered the final authority), social workers sometimes have a hard time having their viewpoint heard or taken seriously. Since social workers' training dictates that they not only look at people's illness or condition, but how that condition may interact with their environment, they may sometimes be the dissenting voice on the team if they do not believe that the patient will be able to adhere to certain treatment. For instance, when treating homeless or impoverished patients, it may be important to evaluate their ability to keep their medications cold if necessary, or if they must be taken with milk, ensuring they have access to milk.

Mental Health

For most mental health positions that have the title social worker attached, an MSW is required. The income for social workers in this field hovered in the mid- to upper $30,000 range in 2004. But based on years of experience, level of position and geographic location, salary could be significantly higher. For instance, within three years of earning a MSW, as a program coordinator of a mental health program at a small nonprofit in New York City, one social worker made over $50,000 per year.

The mental health field offers a variety of career tracks. Whether you work for a small community mental health program or a large hospital determines how much of a promotion you can get.

In smaller CBOs or nonprofits there may be fewer opportunities for promotion, only because there are fewer levels of staff. With a BSW, in the mental health field you can be hired as a counselor or case manager, but for anything higher a Master's degree is typically preferred. If you are at a smaller agency and want to move to a higher-level position, your only option may be moving agencies altogether. If you want to stay at your job but want to gain better skills, you can invest in further training and education, including going back to school for a master's degree, attending a post-graduation program with a specific focus on mental health counseling, working towards an advanced certification in mental

Visit Vault at **www.vault.com** for insider company profiles, expert advice, career message boards, expert resume reviews, the Vault Job Board and more.

VAULT CAREER LIBRARY

77

health or even attending training institutes that teach psychoanalysis. These programs will enhance your skills, broaden your learning base and give your more options to choose from when working with your clients.

Within the mental health field, you may find it difficult to remain at the counselor level without any added administrative or supervisory duties. This is because many social workers are hired to perform the dual role of administrator and clinician, which also brings a higher salary. So if you want to be strictly a counselor, you may have to be willing to take a lesser salary.

Salaries for inpatient mental health settings were around $36,000 in 2004. But the actual salaries within this field vary greatly. One social worker at a state psychiatric hospital in New York City had a starting salary of about $45,000, but after 14 years he made over $75,000 and retired well before age 65 with the additional income generated by his private practice. As an administrator of such a hospital, the salary can begin in the high $90,000s to low $100,000 range. This is a position that requires years of experience as a clinician, as well as skills as an effective administrator.

Mental health social work: pluses and minuses

As with the other fields, there are pros and cons to working in mental health. For starters, you have to accept that your clients will not get better. This is not to say that with medication and proper therapeutic treatment clients are able to function to a higher degree than if these were not in place, but it means that they will never be un-schizophrenic. Once they are diagnosed, they will always be diagnosed. At some points they may be doing really well and then without reason decompensate, or their mental illness symptoms will become very apparent and impair their ability to function.

On the pro side, you are a guide, assisting people to live to their fullest capabilities by helping them stick to their regiments, find jobs, live in apartments in the community and develop meaningful relationships with others.

Substance Abuse

Major service provisions in this role include: diagnosis of substance use as an addiction; treatment recommendations, including replacement therapies like methadone and referrals to inpatient programs; outreach to where substance users are known to congregate to engage them in services; counseling during treatment; and reporting to law enforcement when necessary for clients who are mandated to programs from the criminal justice system. Social workers in this field can work at inpatient programs (where patients live while receiving treatment) at hospitals or treatment facilities, or outpatient plans in nonprofits, community treatment services and clinics affiliated with hospitals. Median salaries for these positions settle in the mid-$30,000 range.

As with many of the other career tracks, the substance use field offers opportunities for advancement to those with experience and the right skills. Since many programs are now based on fees from either insurance programs like Medicaid or other government sponsored dollars, it is important for those at the management level to have some understanding of insurance billing in order to make sure the program has enough operating dollars. In middle management positions, social workers may become supervisors to the actual substance use counselors who are seeing patients. This may put you a step away from the direct service work, but it allows you to guide others in the helping process. What some social workers in these positions do is reserve a limited number of difficult cases for themselves in order to stay connected with the work. These clients may have cases that are more complex, including lengthier drug use histories, a mental health diagnosis, difficult family issues or health issues, all of which require more intensive work with a seasoned clinician that will help clients achieve more positive lifestyles.

Substance abuse: pluses and minuses

Those who work in the field must deal with the behavior associated with substance use, as well as the possibility that a client will return to using and may overdose as a result. On the plus side, those clients who are able to better manage or completely stop their drug use and the negative behaviors associated with it can be a source of accomplishment for the worker. A social worker's support makes it possible for clients to believe that there is a better way to live their lives that may not involve using drugs.

Clinical Social Work

Salaries for clinical social workers vary greatly depending on the position and industry they are working in. Since clinical social workers can be found in all of the aforementioned positions, those salary standards hold. But clinical social workers can also be found in private practice. Because of their specialized training in therapeutic approaches that are helpful to those struggling with a host of different circumstances, from divorce to eating disorders, depression, stress, and rape and sexual assault, clinical social workers are uniquely poised to

Visit Vault at **www.vault.com** for insider company profiles, expert advice, career message boards, expert resume reviews, the Vault Job Board and more.

VAULT CAREER LIBRARY   79

become self-employed through opening their own practices. The going rate for private therapy is $125 per hour, but most clinicians also accept third-party payments from insurance companies at whatever their going rates are.

This career track offers the social worker the flexibility to decide with whom and on what issues she want to work, what hours she will work and how much she will charge for their services. It also allows her to explore other income options, such as providing clinical supervision to other social workers. If a social worker is an expert in a particular issue such as trauma, he may be contracted by agencies to train its staff in the use of trauma-based counseling techniques. Additionally, with the growing popularity of "life coaches," some social workers may decide to expand their practice area to offer coaching services to people who feel stunted in their career or home lives. The Institute for Life Coach Training offers more information on choosing this option, and schools such as the Illinois Network of Charter Schools hire social workers as life coaches to perform regular school social work duties, but also help students develop good character through teaching and modeling responsibility to community.

Government

In addition to working directly with clients, social workers may also head departments of health, alcohol and substance abuse, emergency preparedness, housing and mental health as director or commissioner. In these positions, they would be responsible for the overall function of the department, its employees and all programs affiliated with it. Budget oversight, advocacy with legislators to enhance services and funding allocation, and policy development are often parts of these jobs. Sometimes these positions are appointed by elected officials, such as mayors and governors, and can be linked to specific political parties.

Employment at state and local government agencies may grow somewhat in response to the increasing needs for public welfare, family services and child protection services. However, many of these services tend to be contracted out to private agencies and community-based nonprofits that are already engaged with these communities and can therefore more easily adapt their services to emerging client/community needs.

Getting into government work may be a challenge if you live in a large city with a lot of bureaucracy. You may have to sign up for a civil service list or know someone within the department you want to work in to hear about any vacancies. But once you get into a government position, it is not generally perceived as difficult to move to other agencies or departments or to be promoted based on merit, as hiring and promoting are based on standard procedures.

The advantage to a government agency is that it is more likely to hire recent graduates; the disadvantage is that the salary reflects this. The salary range for government social work runs wide depending on the grade level of your position, with beginning salaries in the low $30,000s to the mid-$40,000s. At the higher levels of executive director or commissioner, you could earn upwards of $80,000 to over $100,000 per year.

Research

The Society for Social Work and Research (SSWR) views social work research as a benefit to consumers, practitioners, policy-makers, educators, and the general public through examining societal issues. These issues include health care; substance abuse and community violence; family issues, including child welfare and aging; wellbeing and resiliency; and the strengths and needs of underserved populations. By exploring the social, behavioral, and environmental connections to health and mental health issues, social work research helps to identify strategies and solutions that enhance individual, family and community wellbeing.

Social work research occurs in schools, communities, health care facilities, and human service agencies. Additionally, social work researchers provide empirical support for best practice approaches to improve service delivery and public policies. The Office of Behavioral and Social Sciences Research (OBSSR), The National Institutes of Health (NIH), the Center for Disease Control and Prevention (CDC) and the National Institute of Justice are a few organizations which offer funding opportunities for social work research in the areas of teen pregnancy, recidivism rates of sex offenders, alcohol use and the effects of domestic violence on women's mental health. The funding amounts vary by agency and can range from a few thousand dollars into the millions, depending on the scope and length of the project. Some of this funding is renewable every year; others are a one-shot deal and require the researcher to reapply as a new candidate each year.

In addition to these organizations, researchers are also employed by nonprofits who want to determine the effectiveness of their services in terms of improving outcomes for clients, or if they can sustain the addition of new programs given their current infrastructure. Some funders, such as the CDC, hire consultant researchers to work with nonprofits to determine whether they are meeting their predetermined objectives.

Determining salaries for this type of position is difficult as many are funded by piecing together money from a number of different sources within an agency. For instance, if the researcher is working on HIV issues, the agency may take

Visit Vault at **www.vault.com** for insider company profiles, expert advice, career message boards, expert resume reviews, the Vault Job Board and more.

V∧ULT CAREER LIBRARY   **81**

monies from each of its programs within its HIV services division to make up the researcher's entire salary. A social worker with 15 years' experience working as a consultant, conducting research on mental health services within an agency to figure out how to better service clients and how to engage more clients in services, could expect to make around $75,000 if the agency's budget is over 10 million dollars. Agencies with smaller budgets are more likely to hire research consultants for a defined period of time, to work on specific issues like how to enhance client flow from one program to another.

Breaking into the research field is usually something you'll want to focus on while in school. When looking for a job, you want to be able to say that you have some experience conducting research, analyzing data or designing research methods. So looking for an internship that offers some hands-on learning in research methods/design is important. Additionally, you may need to decide which area of research you want to focus on: is it design, implementation or data collecting? Being clear about this will also help to focus your job search. If you aren't interested in participant research where you may be talking to survey respondents in person, then jobs like interviewer, survey conductor and primary researcher may not be positions you want to apply for. But if you like to crunch numbers on the back end, then an analyst position might be interesting to you. SSWR offers job postings relevant to this career track as well as helpful information resources.

Research: pluses and minuses

In this field of practice, you may not be able to find a job conducting research on the issue or with the population of your choice, based on how current funding is allocated or what is deemed a pressing issue. If, for instance, your primary interest is in alcohol use among middle-aged men who earn $75,000 per year or more, you may find it difficult to locate a study or funding, since there likely will not be a high demand for this type of work. However, if your interest is in studying the effects of social work services on improving the health outcomes for persons with medical and behavioral disorders and conditions, you will find significant funding opportunities from places like the NIH.

Nonprofit

The most common type of social work practice within nonprofits is casework or case management. Tasks associated with this role include coordinating communication between clients, their caregivers and other service providers, the goal being the provision of services that are consistent throughout, so the client does not receive mixed messages from anyone they are meeting with. These positions often carry with them a lot of paperwork, which is necessary to prove to whoever is funding the program that the client is adequately progressing in treatment, is complying with his treatment regime or is being dutiful in looking for work, housing or monetary support. Salaries in direct service positions can vary greatly based on the size of the agency's fiscal budget, the location of the program and where the money to run it comes from. A reasonable range for this type of work is from $31,000 to $46,000.

As managers, administrators, supervisors, program directors and coordinators, social workers are influencing how organizations operate from within. A program coordinator may be responsible for providing weekly supervision to up to five case managers, offering guidance on their work with clients, including different ways to approach clients that would increase those clients' willingness to look for housing. A coordinator may also be responsible for ensuring that the work being done is within the parameters of the agency's policies on client treatment and staff conduct. As heads of these programs, social workers are responsible for providing program oversight, which may include staff supervision, budget responsibility, policy development to ensure the highest standards of practice are being met, or starting a program from scratch, including assessing a program's needs through focus groups and writing policy and procedures to be followed by all staff and clients. Often included in these positions are employee relations, such as hiring and maintaining a productive work environment. Salaries for these positions range from the low $40s for lower-level supervisory positions and can go up to over $100,000 for senior-level management positions, such as executive directors.

Remember that salaries in nonprofits for social workers are based upon the funding source and the job title. In 2004, the median income for social workers not in a specialized field was $39,440; the middle 50 percent earned between $30,350 and $50,530. The top 10 percent made more than $62,750.

Nonprofits: pluses and minuses

Although there is something of a trend towards hiring lower-skilled workers at reduced salaries to perform some basic social work tasks, such as preliminary evaluation for services and client enrollment, there is no shortage of positions for social workers in this area. The specialized training social workers receive in master's programs, which now often includes not only how to work directly with clients but also areas like budgeting, program development and management practices, combined with the relatively new

Visit Vault at www.vault.com for insider company profiles, expert advice, career message boards, expert resume reviews, the Vault Job Board and more.

VAULT CAREER LIBRARY   83

state licensure requirements, has resulted in many qualified social workers performing higher functions within agencies, often in management positions. In turn, this leaves lower-level positions open for those with associate's and bachelor's degrees. Although these higher-level positions limit contact with clients, they do bring increased salaries and benefits. It is not uncommon to find the majority of supervisory or management staff at nonprofit human service agencies, and the heads of some state and city government agencies, to be social workers. It's possible that in the near future, a social worker's ability to move up within an organization may be limited without an MSW.

Other Opportunities

Social workers are everywhere and the field keeps expanding. You'll still find the majority of social workers in the traditional settings just described, but increasingly social workers inhabit such new and diverse arenas as authors, researchers, politicians and teachers. Furthermore, social work lends itself to multiple positions and not being tied down to traditional 9-to-5 jobs. It is not uncommon for social workers to have two or three more flexible jobs that allow them to either work from home, have minimal office time or require extensive travel to different locales. These opportunities include:

Fee-for-service work

Social workers may be hired per-hour for fees generally between $25 to $45, usually in community mental health programs in the areas of trauma, depression or other mental illness where they'll meet with clients for approximately 45-minute appointments. For the most part, these positions are held by clinical social workers who have experience in the specified area.

Mediators

Courts will often use mediators in lieu of attorneys when one or both parties cannot afford an attorney or if the court feels the dispute can be settled without a court trial. Both parties agree to abide by whatever decision the mediator sets forth and it is legally binding. Social workers' skills translate easily to this position.

One of the best ways to enter this field is to become a volunteer community mediator. John Jay College of Criminal Justice in New York City offers an online manual with tips on becoming a mediator. You can also look for the

Alternative Dispute Resolution Center (ADR) in your county for specific requirements. Nonprofits such as Safe Horizon also offer opportunities for training and gaining experience as a mediator. Once you are properly trained and have some experience, you may even decide to begin your own mediation/dispute resolution practice and charge clients fees for mediating their divorce, child custody, property damage, or workplace incidents. Fees can range from $200-$800 per case/session.

These types of positions are an example of the flexibility in the social work field. You can work a regular full-time job and still do fee-for-service work a couple of hours a week. This work also allows social workers in administrative positions to remain connected to the clinical side of the profession.

Professors

Social workers can become teachers or professors in areas related to social work, or in something completely different. PhD-level social workers are most often hired at the college level for teaching, while those with a master's degree can easily work in undergraduate programs. Most major universities require tenure-track professors to be involved in some type of research or be a recognized authority in a certain topic such as child therapy in order to be published in peer-reviewed journals. Again, this type of job allows the flexibility to do other income-producing jobs that may involve direct client contact, or you can consult in a particular area, providing training to agencies.

Visit Vault at **www.vault.com** for insider company profiles, expert advice, career message boards, expert resume reviews, the Vault Job Board and more.

V/\ULT CAREER LIBRARY   85

Days in the Life

Below are stories from actual social workers in various fields who have practiced for as few as two years, and as many as 15.

Assertive Community Treatment

Christine is an assertive community treatment social worker (ACT) in metropolitan New York. Her employer is a community-based social service agency that works primarily to end homelessness for low-income persons and families, many of whom suffer from mental illness and/or HIV/AIDS.

ACT uses a team approach to provide comprehensive, community-based psychiatric treatment, rehabilitation, and support to persons with serious and persistent mental illness, such as schizophrenia. Many of these teams are available 24 hours a day, seven days a week though a rotating on-call system. Teams are generally made up of interdisciplinary professionals including social workers, rehabilitation specialists, substance use or mental health counselors, nurses and psychiatrists. Teams are run by state mental health hospitals or departments of mental health, such as the Albany County Mental Health in New York or the North Care Center in Oklahoma.

Christine has a bachelor's in teaching and a master's in social work from Hunter College. She's been in the field for three years and her current salary is $44,000.

An average day for Christine is an unpredictable combination of in-office visits, home visits with clients and impromptu hospital stops. Christine's clients are all diagnosed with severe mental illnesses, such as schizophrenia or bipolar disorder, and either live in apartments of their own or in other arrangements for homeless people. During her visits, Christine must assess all clients for their level of mental functioning, make sure they are able to manage the responsibilities of living alone and caring for themselves, and that they are adhering to any prescribed medication treatment. If clients are unable to manage these areas, she can recommend that they receive more intensive services from the team's psychiatrist, possibly a medication adjustment or that they be hospitalized until stable.

7:30 a.m.: Leave for work.

9:00 a.m.: Check voice and e-mail messages for any changes to daily schedule; review daily schedule.

9:30 a.m.: Home visit with client, a 50-year-old man diagnosed with schizophrenia and alcoholism. For the past six years, Hector has been having frequent blackouts as a result of his mixing large quantities of alcohol with his prescribed medications. During these blackouts, Hector has reported having lost money, being beaten up and not being able to remember how he ended up in certain places. During their visits, Christine counsels Hector on his alcohol use and how it interferes with his psychiatric medications.

11:30 a.m.: Meet client at a shelter for Section 8 housing hearing. Roger has been living at a homeless shelter for men for the past eight months and is awaiting approval for a housing subsidy. Because of his disorganized lifestyle, Roger has not been able to properly complete all of the paperwork necessary to complete his application packet. Christine explains the hearing process and what will be expected of Roger throughout the process, as well as what the possible outcomes might be.

12:45 p.m.: Pick up lunch at a drive-through on the way back to the office.

1:00 p.m.: Money management meeting with three clients.

2:30 p.m.: Check voicemail and email messages; write case notes of home visits and in-office meetings with clients from yesterday; prepare notes and presentation for team meeting on all clients, including updates on their housing status, any mental health concerns and overall wellbeing.

3:30 p.m.: Team meeting with co-workers to discuss client progress and updates, review agency policy and procedures, discuss any emerging trends in client care, service population, and work on team building.

4:45 p.m.: Make schedule for tomorrow; return phone calls.

Counselor

James works at a community-based mental health program in New Jersey with clients who have AIDS and may also have a mental illness. In addition to providing direct counseling to clients, James coordinates the program, so his administrative duties include writing monthly reports, maintaining the budget, supervising staff, planning the program's activities and making sure the program achieves its yearly goals. This position also includes facilitating support groups on topics such as self-esteem, substance use, coping with mental illness and building positive interpersonal relationships, as well as conducting individual sessions with clients to help them cope with their HIV status and mental or physical health.

James has a master's in social work and has been in the field for a year-and-a-half. His salary is $52,000.

7:30 a.m.: Commute to work.

8:45 a.m.: Prepare for staff supervision; prepare for groups-decide on topic and write prompting questions/ideas to keep the group focused and interactive, make/copy handouts, prepare flip chart, create sign-in sheet, count transit cards to be given at end of group; review daily schedule.

9:15 a.m.: Supervision with staff (MSW counselor). Agenda for supervision: update on client progress towards goals; discuss any barriers to meeting goals or difficult situations that have arisen; discuss any newly enrolled clients and distribute them to staff; plan activities for the following month; prepare group topics and introduce new ideas; provide guidance on clinical issues related to counseling such as transference, how to help clients reach goals, what therapeutic techniques could be helpful to clients.

10:30 a.m.: 45-minute session with client suffering feelings of helplessness over failing health of her husband and her youngest son's failing marriage and recent incarceration.

11:30 a.m.: One-and-a-half-hour intake session with a new client, assessing him for program enrollment

1:00 p.m.: Lunch.

2:00 p.m.: Hour session with client managing symptoms of schizophrenia, major depression with psychotic features and anxiety disorder. Counsel client on understanding each of his disorders and how they affect his everyday life (what feelings/behaviors can be attributed to his disorders, how to cope when he begins to feel overwhelmed). Review prescription medication regime.

3:00 p.m.: Facilitate men's group. Topic: Men and HIV-what does being diagnosed with HIV mean to your manhood? The group discusses traditional roles of men in American society and how interpretation of these roles may have led to their infection, and how they play into their treatment.

4:15 p.m.: 45-minute session with client dealing with recent rapid health decline from AIDS.

Consultant

Visit Vault at **www.vault.com** for insider company profiles, expert advice, career message boards, expert resume reviews, the Vault Job Board and more.

VAULT CAREER LIBRARY   **89**

Emily provides consulting services to family and child services programs that assist children who have been victims of sexual assault or physical abuse. She started her own consulting business about two years ago after 12 years of working with children, adults and families who have experienced abuse. She interviews children of all ages in what are considered high-profile abuse cases. Additionally, she maintains a private practice counseling adult victims of child abuse.

Emily lives in San Francisco. She has a master's in psychology and a master's in social work. She's been in the field for 15 years and makes $101,000.

10:00 a.m.: Meeting with city child services office for briefing on a new case of assault and perimeters of involvement.

12:00 p.m.: Lunch meeting with private child services agency to assist in curriculum development for a new child abuse prevention/recognition program they are developing.

2:30 p.m.: Interview with nine-year-old boy alleging sexual assault by father; follow-up debriefing with police, district attorney, child protective services and mother.

5:00 p.m.: Phone check-in at office with support staff; next day schedule, important messages, authorize payroll.

5:30 p.m.: Grab food at drive-through on way to private counseling office.

6:00 p.m.: Two one-hour counseling sessions.

8:00 p.m.: Write notes.

Case Manager

Cynthia works in Boston as a case manager with homeless clients, helping them in securing public assistance, housing subsidies and other needs to maintain that housing. She has a bachelor's in social work and has been in the field for two years. Her salary is $32,000.

9:00 a.m.: Check voice-mail; complete case notes from the previous day; write schedule.

10:00 a.m.: Meeting with client, but client does not show up for appointment.

10:30 a.m.: Unscheduled meeting with client; complete housing subsidy paperwork; phone call to local shelter to secure bed for the night; provide a meal voucher.

11:45 a.m.: Intake interview with potential client, but after half an hour realize client is not eligible because he has the option of staying with family outside of city.

12:30 p.m.: Eat lunch while on the phone with public assistance to advocate for several clients to receive their rent checks on time to move into apartments by the first of the month.

2:00 p.m.: Home visit with client.

3:45 p.m.: Supervision with program coordinator, review of current cases and suggestions on how to proceed.

4:30 p.m.: Review of files for correct and up-to-date paperwork.

5:00 p.m.: Write and mail four letters to clients without contact for two weeks or more.

School Social Worker

Jamal works for the Albany, N.Y. city school district as a social worker at a junior high school. He has a master's in social work and has been in the field six years. His salary is $45,000.

8:00 a.m.: Arrive at office and prepare for the day. Check voice-mail and consult appointment book.

8:45 a.m.: Meeting with school principal about setting up a new school-based initiative on drug abuse.

10:00 a.m.: Meeting with a 12-year-old girl with history of domestic violence at home.

10:30 a.m.: Conduct a classroom learning session with students on healthy self-esteem and building positive self-image.

11:30 a.m.: Again, facilitate self-esteem program in classrooms.

12:00 p.m.: Lunch in teacher's room; impromptu meetings with students in lunchroom.

1:30 p.m.: More facilitation of self-esteem program in classrooms.

Visit Vault at **www.vault.com** for insider company profiles, expert advice, career message boards, expert resume reviews, the Vault Job Board and more.

VAULT CAREER LIBRARY   **91**

3:00 p.m.: Write notes on today's interactions; contact parents for meetings and to discuss concerns about their children; prepare for conference with parents of one child concerned about his declining grades and withdrawn attitude.

APPENDIX

Buzz Words

As with any industry, there are certain words or terms that are unique to the social work profession. You should familiarize yourself with them, and use them in your resume and during interviews.

ACT: An evidence-based, outreach-oriented, service-delivery model that provides comprehensive, locally-based treatment to people with serious and persistent mental illnesses.

Assessment: Evaluation of an individual, family or group's personal, social, health or behavior problems through interviews, records review and/or testing to determine what services are necessary.

Case management: Basic social work involving assessing needs and applying agency services and resources to address social, health or economic problems, such as homelessness, HIV/AIDS and job skills training. These services can be offered in health, community agencies and public welfare programs.

Clinical social work: found in private practice or in psychiatric and mental health care settings, where they provide psychotherapy and counseling. They might also work in employee assistance programs (EAP) where they would meet with employees a few times to determine if more intensive therapy or other treatment options are warranted.

Community-based organization (CBO): as a non-profit (see nonprofit), generally designed to serve the disadvantaged in the community in which it is located.

Community organizing: work in cooperation with the community to identify needs and to develop or improve services and systems to meet those needs. Organization of immigrant community members for the improvement of working conditions, increase of English as a second language (ESL) courses and legislation that impacts immigrants are examples of community organizing work.

Congregate housing: shared multiunit housing for seniors and adults with mental and/or physical disabilities who do not want to or cannot live alone. Congregate housing offers support services to help residents remain independent, including prepared meals, transportation, housekeeping, building security, case management, nursing services and social activities. A congregate coordinator evaluates resident's appropriateness for services.

Consultant: a person who provides expert services on a particular area, subject or services. An agency hires this person to develop or enhance its

Visit Vault at **www.vault.com** for insider company profiles, expert advice, career message boards, expert resume reviews, the Vault Job Board and more.

V/\ULT CAREER LIBRARY   95

current services as it generally does not have a current staff person with this expertise.

Counseling: the interpersonal helping relationship between client and social worker that begins with the clients exploring the way they think, how they feel and what they do for the purpose of enhancing their life and creating positive change.

Counter-transference: refers to the therapists' feelings about the clients that stem from the therapists' own life experiences and issues, where therapists begin to transfer their own repressed feelings to the patient.

Day treatment: structured services for individuals with mental health or developmental disabilities generally including recreational/social skills, daily living skills, rehabilitation and therapy.

Deinstitutionalization: a series of health care policy reforms that began in the 1970s that shifted mental health care from dependence on public hospitals to community-based programs. During this time, hundreds of people were discharged from psychiatric institutions under the idea that with proper management of their psychiatric medications, behavior modification and monitoring, these patients could live independently in the community. Many communities and former patients were not equipped to handle this change, and social workers were called upon to act as educators and liaisons between the community and the former patients, teaching each the skills necessary to cope in their new environments.

Direct service: the most common type of social work practice, this term describes any work directly with a client, including counseling, assessment of client needs and evaluation for services.

Discharge planning: the determination of a patient's needs for returning home after inpatient treatment for medical or psychiatric purposes. It may include structural accommodations for the home, in-home nursing services, assessment of family members ability to care for the patient and possible placement in a care facility.

Dual Diagnosis: occurs when an individual is affected by both chemical dependency and psychiatric/emotional illness. At times the symptoms can overlap and even mask each other, making treatment and diagnosis difficult. To fully recover, a person needs to treat/address both disorders. CAMI (chemically addicted and mentally ill) and MICA (mentally ill, chemically addicted) and "double trouble" are often used interchangeable to describe a dually diagnosed person.

Ecological model: a comprehensive health promotion model that takes into account the physical environment and its relationship to people at individual, organizational and community levels. The belief is that behavior does not occur in a vacuum, so in order to effect change all external and internal factors must be taken into account.

Emergency assistance: the provision of immediate, short-term assistance for individuals and families in a financial and/or housing crisis.

Empathy: commonly defined as one's ability to recognize, perceive and directly feel the emotion of another.

Engagement: beginning with the first contact and continuing throughout the client-worker relationship, this process aims to clarify the helping process for the client, develop the foundation for a collaborative working relationship, and problem solve around identified barriers to help-seeking.

Follow-up care: the continued provision of services after a client is discharge from primary care services by an agency. For instance, after being housed clients may remain in case management services to help them successfully maintain their housing.

Geriatric social work: a field of social work concentrating on work with the elderly.

Grant funding: the provision of monies to nonprofits contingent on the successful rendering of services to clients based on specific outcomes, such as the number of clients served, type of services provided and length of time clients remain in the program. If programs fail to meet the outcomes the funding can be revoked and the program shut down.

Group Work: some social workers work with people in groups to effect change. These groups can be exclusive to members of a single family or they can consist of unrelated people who have a common issue or need such as Alcoholics Anonymous, cancer survivor groups, teen parents and sexual assault survivors.

Harm reduction: a set of practical strategies that reduce negative consequences of drug use, incorporating a spectrum of strategies from safer use, to managed use to abstinence. Harm reduction strategies meet drug users "where they're at," addressing conditions of use along with the use itself.

Holistic: In social work context, treating the whole person rather than just the symptoms of their disease, ailment or current issue; looking at the whole system (family, life circumstances, current relationships, physical/mental/emotional health) rather than just concentrating on individual components.

Hospice care: services for terminally ill patients and their families, including counseling, palliative care, daily hygiene, medication management and other end of life services. These services can be rendered in a facility or at home.

Visit Vault at **www.vault.com** for insider company profiles, expert advice, career message boards, expert resume reviews, the Vault Job Board and more.

V/\ULT CAREER LIBRARY **97**

Indirect service: in these positions, the social worker may not have direct contact with the client or build a relationship with them. Some examples are program administrators, researchers, consultants who work with agencies to help improve their work with clients. At insurance companies, social workers may talk to members and decide whether to approve a certain treatment option

Intake: process of assessing a potential client's needs and eligibility for service.

Intervention: Becoming involved or advocating for a client to increase their safety and wellbeing.

Not-for-profit (nonprofit): a club, society, agency, or association organized and operated solely for social welfare, civic improvement, pleasure or recreation, or for any other purpose than profit.

Outreach services: a systematic attempt to provide services beyond conventional limits to particular segments of a community, such as the homeless, minorities and poor communities.

Person in environment (theory of practice): a framework social workers use to describe client problems as an interaction of the person (the client) and their surroundings (family, neighborhood, place of birth, workplace etc.)

Process recording: a social work student's written assessment of interaction with clients including the actual encounter, clinical impressions of the client and any unresolved clinical or personal issues about the encounter/client. The client's supervisor reviews this document and uses in the provision of clinical supervision to the student.

Psychosocial assessment: evaluation taking into account a person's mental and physical functioning, health, family history and current living conditions.

Psychotherapy: a range of techniques based on dialogue, communication and behavior change designed to improve the mental health of a client or patient, or to improve group relationships (such as in a family).

Self-determination: one of the ethical principles of social work practice that recognizes the client's right to make his own choices even if they are counter to the social worker's advice.

SPMI: Seriously and Persistently Mentally Ill; persons in this category generally have severe forms of schizophrenia and are unable to manage their personal lives without professional intervention or institutionalization.

Supportive counseling: a less intensive form of therapeutic counseling based on the needs presented by the client and not on a particular disorder. Used mostly with those who have experienced traumatic events, have mild depression, physical illnesses, disorders and diseases other then severe psychiatric disorders.

Transference: a client's transferring of feelings of people in their life to the therapist.

Visit Vault at **www.vault.com** for insider company profiles, expert advice, career message boards, expert resume reviews, the Vault Job Board and more.

VAULT CAREER LIBRARY   99

Credentials and Certifications

The National Association of Social Workers (NASW) supports and administers the following specialty credentials and certifications for social workers in specialized fields and with specific years of practice. For more information visit the NASW web site at www.naswdc.org/credentials.

Qualified Clinical Social Worker (QCSW)

This national credential is available to social workers who are current members of NASW, earned an MSW from an accredited school, completed at least 3,000 hours or two years of documented postgraduate supervised clinical experience and hold a current state social work license.

Diplomate in Clinical Social Work (DCSW)

Those who hold a DCSW are recognized in the profession as providers of behavioral health care. This is the highest NASW-sponsored distinction available to clinical social workers. In order to qualify for this level of credentialing you must: be a current NASW member, hold an MSW from an accredited program, have documented five years of postgraduate clinical social work experience, completed 20 hours of clinical case work, provide professional evaluations that validate your interpersonal skills, clinical practice skills, ethical standards of social work practice form an MSW supervisor, have a current membership in the ACSW or hold a clinical license and agree to adhere to NASW code of ethics, standards of practice and standards for continuing professional education.

Academy of Certified Social Workers (ACSW)

ACSW was established in 1960 and remains the most widely recognized and respected social work credential. Social workers who hold the ACSW are qualified providers of social services. To qualify NASW members must provide professional evaluations that validate their knowledge, understanding, and application of social work principles and values from an MSW supervisor and two social work colleagues; verified 20 hours of relevant continuing education.

Other specialty NASW-sponsored certifications include:

MSW

- *Clinical Social Worker in Gerontology (CSW-G):* geared for clinical social workers who work directly with older adults.

- *Advanced Social Worker in Gerontology (ASW-G):* distinguishes macro-administrative social workers in the field of aging.

- *Certified Advanced Children, Youth and Family Social Worker (C-ACYFSW):* highlights social workers who promote the well-being of children and families.

- *Certified Social Worker in Health Care (C-SWHC):* distinguishes social workers in a multi-disciplinary healthcare environment.

- *Certified Clinical Alcohol, Tobacco and Other Drugs Social Worker (C-CATODSW):* recognizes highly trained social workers in the substance abuse field

- *Certified Advanced Social Work Case Manager (C-ASWCM):* establishes social workers as professionals in a variety of work settings.

- *Certified School Social Work Specialist (C-SSWS):* identifies social workers who specialize within a school system.

BSW

- *Social Worker in Gerontology (SW-G):* recognizes care and case management professionalism in work with older adults.

- *Certified Children, Youth, and Family Social Worker (C-CYFSW):* gives credibility to professionally trained children, youth, and family social workers.

- *Certified Social Work Case Manager (C-SWCM):* highlights the professional standing of social workers.

Recommended Reading

Social Work Journals

- *Journal of Dual Diagnosis*, research and practice in substance abuse comorbidity. The Haworth Medical Press and The Haworth Press, Inc.

- *Journal of Family Social Work*, Haworth Press, Inc.

- *The Journal of Supervision in Psychotherapy & Mental Health: The Clinical Supervisor*. The Haworth Social Work Practice Press.

- *The New Social Worker.com:* an online magazine for social workers

- *NASWpress online journals:*
  Social Work
  Health and Social Work
  Social Work Research
  Children and Schools

Mental Illness and Substance Use

Beck, Aaron and Emery, Gary. *Anxiety Disorders and Phobias: A Cognitive Perspective.* Basic Books, 1985.

Daley, Dennis C. and Moss, Howard B.. *Dual Disorders: Counseling Clients with Chemical*

Dependency and Mental Illness (third edition). Minnesota: Hazelden, 2002.

Jamison, Kay Redfield. *An Unquiet Mind: A memoir of moods and madness.* New York: Vintage Books, 1996.

Lickey, Marvin E. and Gordon, Barbara. Medicine and Mental Illness: *The use of drugs in psychiatry.* New York: W.H Freeman and Company, 1991.

Papolos, Demitri; Papolos, Janice. *Overcoming Depression (revised edition).* New York: HarperCollins Publishers, 1992.

Rapoport, Juditih, L. *The Boy who Couldn't Stop Washing: The experience and treatment of obsessive compulsive disorder.* New York: Signet, 1991.

Rubin, Allen and Babbie, Earl. *Research Methods for Social Work (fourth edition).* Wadsworth, 2001.

Sadock, Benjamin James and Sadock, Virginia Alcott. *Kaplin and Sadock's Synopsis of Psychiatry: Behavioral Sciences/Clinical Psychiatry 9th edition.* Pennsylvania: Lippincott Williams and Wilkins, 2003.

Torrey, E. Fuller. *Surviving Schizophrenia: A manual for families, consumers and providers (fourth edition).* New York: HarperCollins, 2001.

Social Work Practice

Best, Joel. *Images of Issues: Typifying Contemporary Social Problems (second edition).* New York: Aldine De Gruyter, 1995.

Martin, Patricia Yancy and O'Connor Gerald G. *The Social Environment: Open Systems Applications.* New York: Longman, 1998.

Miley, Karla Krogsrud, O'Melia, Michael and Dubois, Brenda. *Generalist Social Work Practice: An Empowering Approach.* Allyn and Bacon, 2001.

Cultural Competence

Foster Perez, RoseMarie; Moskowitz, Micheal; Javier, Rafael Art. *Reaching Across Boundaries of Culture and Class: Widening the Scope of Psychotherapy.* New Jersey: Jason Aronson, Inc. 1996

Andersen, Margaret L. and Hill Collins, Patricia. *Race, Class and Gender: An anthology (fourth edition).* Wadsworth, 2001.

Sexual Abuse

Bass, Ellen and Thornton, Louise. *I Never Told Anyone: Writings by women survivors of child sexual abuse.* New York: Harper Perennial, 1991.

Gartner, Richard B. *Betrayed as Boys: Psychodynamic Treatment of Sexually Abused Men.* New York: The Guildford Press, 1999.

Poverty

Kusmer, Kenneth L. *Down and Out on the Road: The Homeless in American History.* New York: Oxford University Press, 2002.

Katz, Michael B. *In the Shadow of the Poorhouse.* Basic Books, 1986.

Trattner, Walter I. *From Poor Law to Welfare State: A History of Social Welfare in America.* New York: Simon & Schuster. 1999

Professional

Simpson, Carolyn and Simpson, Dwain. *Careers in Social Work.* New York: The Rosen Publishing Group, Inc, 1999.

Visit Vault at **www.vault.com** for insider company profiles, expert advice, career message boards, expert resume reviews, the Vault Job Board and more.

VAULT CAREER LIBRARY   **105**

Schools of Social Work

See www.cswe.org for the most up-to-date and comprehensive listings of accredited social work programs.

Master's of Social Work Programs

Alabama

Alabama A&M University
Social Work Department
P.O. Box 1417
Normal, AL 35762
Phone: (256) 372-5478
Fax: (256) 372-5484

University of Alabama
School of Social Work
Box 870314
Tuscaloosa, AL 35487-0314
Phone: (205) 348-7027
Fax: (205) 348-9419

Alaska

University of Alaska Anchorage
School of Social Work
College of Health and Social Welfare
3211 Providence Drive
Anchorage, AK 99508-8230
Phone: (907) 786-6900
Fax: (907) 786-6912

Arizona

Arizona State University, Tempe Campus
School of Social Work
Box 871802
Tempe, AZ 85287-1802
Phone: (480) 965-2795
Fax: (480) 965-2799

Arizona State University, West Campus
Department of Social Work
College of Human Services-MC: 3251
P.O. Box 3251
Phoenix, AZ 85069-7100
Phone: (602) 543-4679
Fax: (602) 543-6612

Arkansas

University of Arkansas
School of Social Work
ASUP 106
Fayetteville, AR 72701
Phone: (479) 575-5039
Fax: (479) 575-4145

University of Arkansas at Little Rock
School of Social Work
2801 S. University Avenue
Little Rock, AR 72204
Phone: (501) 569-3240
Fax: (501) 569-3184

California

California State University, Bakersfield
Social Work Program
9001 Stockdale Highway
Bakersfield, CA 93311-1099
Phone: (661) 664-3434
Fax: (661) 665-6928

California State University, Long Beach
Department of Social Work

Visit Vault at **www.vault.com** for insider company profiles, expert advice, career message boards, expert resume reviews, the Vault Job Board and more.

VAULT CAREER LIBRARY   **107**

1250 Bellflower Boulevard
Long Beach, CA 90840-4602
Phone: (562) 985-4684
Fax: (562) 985-5514

California State University, Los Angeles
School of Social Work
5151 State University Drive
Los Angeles, CA 90008
Phone: (323) 343-4680
Fax: (323) 343-6312

California State University, Sacramento
Division of Social Work
6000 J Street
Sacramento, CA 95819-6090
Phone: (916) 278-6943
Fax: (916) 278-7167

San Diego State University
School of Social Work
5500 Campanile Drive
San Diego, CA 92182-4119
Phone: (619) 594-6865
Fax: (619) 594-5991

San Francisco State University
School of Social Work
1600 Holloway Avenue
San Francisco, CA 94132
Coordinator
Phone: (415) 338-1003
Fax: (415) 338-0591

University of California at Berkeley
School of Social Welfare
120 Haviland Hall
Berkeley, CA 94720-7400
Phone: (510) 642-4341
Fax: (510) 643-6126

University of California at Los Angeles
Department of Social Welfare
School of Public Policy and Social
Research

3250 Public Policy Building, Box 951656
Los Angeles, CA 90095-1656
Phone: (310) 825-2892
Fax: (310) 206-7564

University of Southern California
School of Social Work
MRF Building, Room 214
699 W. 34th St.
Los Angeles, CA 90089-0411
Phone: (213) 740-2711
Fax: (213) 740-3301

Colorado

Colorado State University
School of Social Work
127 Education Building
Fort Collins, CO 80523-1586
Phone: (970) 491-2536
Fax: (970) 491-7280

University of Denver
Graduate School of Social Work
2148 S. High Street
Denver, CO 80208-2886
Phone: (303) 871-2203
Fax: (303) 871-2845

Connecticut

Southern Connecticut State University
Graduate Social Work Program
Department of Social Work
101 Farnham Avenue
New Haven, CT 06515
Phone: (203) 392-6551
Fax: (203) 392-6580

University of Connecticut
School of Social Work
1798 Asylum Avenue
West Hartford, CT 06117
Phone: (860) 570-9141
Fax: (860) 570-9264

Delaware

Delaware State University
Master of Social Work Program
Department of Social Work
1200 N. DuPont Highway
Dover, DE 19901
Phone: (302) 857-6770
Fax: (302) 857-6794

District of Columbia

Catholic University of America
National Catholic School of Social Service
Shahan Hall-Cardinal Station
Washington, DC 20064
Phone: (202) 319-5458
Fax: (202) 319-5093

Howard University
School of Social Work
601 Howard Place, NW
Washington, DC 20059
Cudore L. Snell, Dean
Phone: (202) 806-7300
Fax: (202) 387-4309

Florida

Florida Agricultural and Mechanical University
Department of Social Work
301 Ware-Rhaney Building
Tallahassee, FL 32307-3500
Phone: (850) 599-3456
Fax: (850) 599-3215

Florida Atlantic University
School of Social Work
777 Glades Road
Boca Raton, FL 33431-0091
Phone: (561) 297-3234
Fax: (561) 297-2866

Florida State University
College of Social Work
UCC 2505
Tallahassee, FL 32306-2570
Phone: (850) 644-4751
Fax: (850) 644-9750

University of Central Florida
School of Social Work
P.O. Box 163358
Orlando, FL 32828
Phone: (407) 823-2114
Fax: (407) 823-5697

University of South Florida
School of Social Work
MGY 132
4202 E. Fowler Avenue
Tampa, FL 33620-8100
Phone: (813) 974-2063
Fax: (813) 974-4675

Georgia

Clark Atlanta University
Whitney M. Young, Jr., School of Social Work
223 James P. Brawley Drive, SW
Atlanta, GA 30314-4391
Phone: (404) 880-8311
Fax: (404) 880-6434

Georgia State University
School of Social Work
College of Health and Human Sciences
MSC 8L0381
33 Gilmer Street, SE Unit 8
Atlanta, GA 30303-3083
Phone: (404) 651-3526
Fax: (404) 651-1863

University of Georgia
School of Social Work
Tucker Hall
Athens, GA 30602-7016

Visit Vault at **www.vault.com** for insider company profiles, expert advice,
career message boards, expert resume reviews, the Vault Job Board and more.

VAULT CAREER LIBRARY   **109**

Phone: (706) 542-3364
Fax: (706) 542-3282

Valdosta State University
Division of Social Work
1500 Patterson Street
Valdosta, GA 31698
Phone: (229) 249-4864
Fax: (229) 245-4341

Idaho

Boise State University
School of Social Work
1910 University Drive
Boise, ID 83725-1940
Phone: (208) 426-1568
Fax: (208) 426-4291

Northwest Nazarene University
Department of Social Work
623 Holly Street
Nampa, ID 83686-5897
Phone: (208) 467-8826
Fax: (208) 467-8879

Illinois

Aurora University
School of Social Work
George Williams College of Health and Human
Services
347 S. Gladstone Avenue
Aurora, IL 60506-4892
Phone: (630) 844-5419
Fax: (630) 844-4923

Chicago State University
Department of Social Work
Williams Science Center 315
9501 S. King Drive
Chicago, IL 60628-1598
Phone: (773) 995-2207
Fax: (773) 821-2420

Governors State University
College of Health Professions
Master's of Social Work Program
University Park, IL 60466
Phone: (708) 235-3997
Fax: (708) 235-2196

Illinois State University
School of Social Work
Campus Box 4650
Normal, IL 61790-4650
Phone: (309) 438-3631
Fax: (309) 438-5880

Loyola University of Chicago
School of Social Work
820 N. Michigan Avenue
Chicago, IL 60611
Phone: (312) 915-7005
Fax: (312) 915-7645

Southern Illinois University Carbondale
School of Social Work
Quigley Hall, Room 6
Mail Code 4329
Carbondale, IL 62901-4329
Phone: (618) 453-2243
Fax: (618) 453-4291

Southern Illinois University Edwardsville
Department of Social Work
College of Arts and Sciences, Peck Hall, Room 1306
P.O. Box 1450
Edwardsville, IL 62026-1450
Phone: (618) 650-5758
Fax: (618) 650-3509

University of Chicago
School of Social Service Administration
969 E. 60th Street
Chicago, IL 60637
Phone: (773) 702-1250
Fax: (773) 834-1582

University of Illinois at Chicago
Jane Addams College of Social Work
M/C 309
1040 W. Harrison Street
Chicago, IL 60607-7134
Phone: (312) 996-3218
Fax: (312) 996-2770

Indiana

Indiana University
School of Social Work
902 W. New York Street
ES 4138
Indianapolis, IN 46202-5156
Phone: (317) 274-6705
Fax: (317) 274-8630

University of Southern Indiana
Social Work Department
8600 University Boulevard
Evansville, IN 47712
Phone: (812) 464-1843
Fax: (812) 465-1116

Iowa

St. Ambrose University
School of Social Work
518 W. Locust Street
Davenport, IA 52803
Phone: (563) 333-6379
Fax: (563) 333-6097

University of Iowa
School of Social Work
308 North Hall
Iowa City, IA 52242-1223
Phone: (319) 335-1250
Fax: (319) 335-1711

Kansas

Newman University
Social Work Program
3100 McCormick Avenue
Wichita, KS 67213-2097
Phone: (316) 942-4291 x216
Fax: (316) 942-4483

University of Kansas
School of Social Welfare
1545 Lilac Lane
Lawrence, KS 66044-3184
Phone: (785) 864-4720
Fax: (785) 864-5277

Wichita State University
School of Social Work
Box 154
1845 Fairmount
Wichita, KS 67620-0154
Phone: (316) 978-7250
Fax: (316) 978-3328

Kentucky

Spalding University
School of Social Work
851 S. Fourth Street
Louisville, KY 40203-2115
Phone: (502) 585-9911 x2183
Fax: (502) 992-2413

University of Kentucky
College of Social Work
619 Patterson Office Tower
Lexington, KY 40506-0027
Phone: (859) 257-6654
Fax: (859) 323-1030

Visit Vault at www.vault.com for insider company profiles, expert advice, career message boards, expert resume reviews, the Vault Job Board and more.

VAULT CAREER LIBRARY   111

Louisiana

Grambling State University
School of Social Work
P.O. Box 907
Grambling, LA 71245
Phone: (318) 274-3166
Fax: (318) 274-3254

Louisiana State University
School of Social Work
311 Huey P. Long Field House
Baton Rouge, LA 70803
Phone: (225) 578-1351
Fax: (225) 578-1357

Tulane University
School of Social Work
6823 St. Charles Avenue
New Orleans, LA 70118-5672
Phone: (504) 865-5314
Fax: (504) 862-8727

Maine

University of Maine
School of Social Work
5770 Social Work Building
Orono, ME 04469
Phone: (207) 581-2389
Fax: (207) 581-2396

University of Southern Maine
Department of Social Work
96 Falmouth Street
P.O. Box 9300
Portland, ME 04104-9300
Vincent E. Faherty, Interim Director
Phone: (207) 780-4227
Fax: (207) 780-4902

Maryland

Salisbury University
Department of Social Work
1101 Camden Avenue
Salisbury, MD 21801
Phone: (410) 543-6305
Fax: (410) 548-2593

University of Maryland-Baltimore
School of Social Work
Louis L. Kaplan Hall
525 W. Redwood Street
Baltimore, MD 21201-1777
Phone: (410) 706-7794
Fax: (410) 706-0273

Massachusetts

Boston College
Graduate School of Social Work
McGuinn Hall
140 Commonwealth Avenue
Chestnut Hill, MA 02467-3807
Phone: (617) 552-4020
Fax: (617) 552-2374

Boston University
School of Social Work
264 Bay State Road
Boston, MA 02215
Phone: (617) 353-3750
Fax: (617) 353-5612

Salem State College
School of Social Work
352 Lafayette Street
Salem, MA 01970
Phone: (978) 542-6650
Fax: (978) 542-6936

Simmons College
School of Social Work
300 The Fenway
Boston, MA 02115

Phone: (617) 521-3900
Fax: (617) 521-3980

Smith College
School for Social Work
Lilly Hall
Northampton, MA 01063
Phone: (413) 585-7950
Fax: (413) 585-7994

Springfield College
School of Social Work
263 Alden Street
Springfield, MA 01109-3797
Phone: (413) 748-3065
Fax: (413) 748-3069

Michigan

Michigan State University
School of Social Work
254 Baker Hall
East Lansing, MI 48824
Phone: (517) 353-8632
Fax: (517) 353-3038

University of Michigan
School of Social Work
1080 S. University
Ann Arbor, MI 48109-1106
Phone: (734) 764-5340
Fax: (734) 764-9954

Minnesota

College of Saint Catherine
Mail LOR 406
2115 Summit Avenue
St Paul, MN 55105
Phone: (651) 962-5810
Fax: (651) 962-5819

University of Minnesota-Duluth
Department of Social Work
220 Bohannon Hall

Duluth, MN 55812-2496
Phone: (218) 726-7245
Fax: (218) 726-7185

University of Minnesota-Twin Cities
School of Social Work
105 Peters Hall
1404 Gortner Avenue
St. Paul, MN 55108
Phone: (612) 625-1220
Fax: (612) 624-3744

University of St. Thomas
Mail LOR 406
2115 Summit Avenue
St Paul, MN 55105
Phone: (651) 962-5810
Fax: (651) 962-5819

Mississippi

Jackson State University
School of Social Work
3825 Ridgewood Road, Suite 9
Jackson, MS 39211
Phone: (601) 432-6819
Fax: (601) 432-6827

University of Southern Mississippi
School of Social Work
Box 5114
Hattiesburg, MS 39406
Phone: (601) 266-4163
Fax: (601) 266-4165

Missouri

Missouri State University
School of Social Work
Professional Building, Suite 200
901 S. National Ave.
Springfield, MO 65804
Phone: (417) 836-6953
Fax: (417) 836-7688

Visit Vault at **www.vault.com** for insider company profiles, expert advice,
career message boards, expert resume reviews, the Vault Job Board and more.

VAULT CAREER LIBRARY   **113**

Saint Louis University
School of Social Work
3550 Lindell Boulevard
St. Louis, MO 63103
Phone: (314) 977-2712
Fax: (314) 977-2731

University of Missouri-St. Louis
School of Social Welfare
College of Arts and Sciences
One University Boulevard
St. Louis, MO 63121-4400
Phone: (314) 516-6385
Fax: (314) 516-5816

Washington University
George Warren Brown School of Social Work
One Brookings Drive
Campus Box 1196
St. Louis, MO 63130-4899
Master's Program
Phone: (314) 935-6693
Fax: (314) 935-8511

Montana

University of Montana
School of Social Work
Jeanette Rankin Hall
Missoula, MT 59812-4392
Phone: (406) 243-5543
Fax: (406) 243-5275

Nebraska

University of Nebraska at Omaha
School of Social Work
Annex 40
60th and Dodge Streets
Omaha, NE 68182-0293
Phone: (402) 554-2793
Fax: (402) 554-3788

Nevada

University of Nevada, Las Vegas
School of Social Work
4505 Maryland Parkway
Box 455032
Las Vegas, NV 89154-5032
Phone: (702) 895-4338
Fax: (702) 895-4079

University of Nevada, Reno
School of Social Work
Business Building, Room 523
Mail Stop 090
Reno, NV 89557-0068
Phone: (775) 784-6542
Fax: (775) 784-4573

New Hampshire

University of New Hampshire
Department of Social Work
Pettee Hall
55 College Road
Durham, NH 03824-3596
Phone: (603) 862-1799
Fax: (603) 862-4374

New Jersey

Monmouth University
Social Work Department
Norwood and Cedar Avenue
West Long Branch, NJ 07764-1898
Phone: (732) 571-3543
Fax: (732) 263-5217

The State University of New Jersey, Rutgers
School of Social Work
536 George Street
New Brunswick, NJ 08901-1167
Phone: (732) 932-7253
Fax: (732) 932-8915

New Mexico

New Mexico State University
School of Social Work
P.O. Box 30001, MSC 3SW
Las Cruces, NM 88003-8001
Phone: (505) 646-2143
Fax: (505-646-4116
E-mail: stephean@nmsu.edu

New York

Adelphi University
School of Social Work
South Avenue
Garden City, NY 11530
Phone: (516) 877-4355
Fax: (516) 877-4436

Columbia University
School of Social Work
1255 Amsterdam Avenue
New York, NY 10027
Phone: (212) 851-2289
Fax: (212) 851-2323

Fordham University
Graduate School of Social Service
113 W. 60th St., Room 726
Lincoln Center Campus
New York, NY 10023-7479
Phone: (212) 636-6600
Fax: (212) 636-7876

Hunter College of the City University
of New York
School of Social Work
129 E. 79th Street
New York, NY 10021
Phone: (212) 452-7085
Fax: (212) 452-7150

New York University
School of Social Work
One Washington Square North
New York, NY 10003
Phone: (212) 998-5959
Fax: (212) 995-4172

State University of New York at Stony Brook
School of Social Welfare
Health Sciences Center
Level 2, Room 093
Stony Brook, NY 11794-8231
Phone: (631) 444-2139
Fax: (631) 444-8908

State University of New York, University at Buffalo
School of Social Work
685 Baldy Hall
Box 601050
Buffalo, NY 14260-1050
Phone: (716) 645-3381 x221
Fax: (716) 645-3883

Syracuse University
School of Social Work
Sims Hall
Syracuse, NY 13244-1230
Phone: (315) 443-5550
Fax: (315) 443-5576

University at Albany, State University of New York
School of Social Welfare
135 Western Avenue
Albany, NY 12222
Phone: (518) 442-5324
Fax: (518) 442-5380

Yeshiva University
Wurzweiler School of Social Work
Belfer Hall
2495 Amsterdam Avenue
New York, NY 10033
Phone: (212) 960-0820
Fax: (212) 960-0822

Visit Vault at www.vault.com for insider company profiles, expert advice, career message boards, expert resume reviews, the Vault Job Board and more.

VAULT CAREER LIBRARY   115

North Carolina

East Carolina University
College of Human Ecology
School of Social Work
Ragsdale Building, Room 104-C
Greenville, NC 27858-4353
Phone: (252) 328-4189
Fax: (252) 328-4196

North Carolina A&T State University
Department of Social Work
P.O. Box 26170
Greensboro, NC 27402-6170
Phone: (336) 334-4100
Fax: (336) 334-5210

University of North Carolina at Chapel Hill
School of Social Work
Tate-Turner-Kuralt Building, CB 3550
301 Pittsboro Street
Chapel Hill, NC 27599-3550
Phone: (919) 962-6532
Fax: (919) 962-3384

University of North Carolina at Charlotte
Master of Social Work Program
9201 University City Boulevard
Charlotte, NC 28223-0001
Phone: (704) 687-4076
Fax: (704) 687-2343

North Dakota

University of North Dakota
Department of Social Work
Gillette Hall
Box 7135
Grand Forks, ND 58202-7135
Phone: (701) 777-2669
Fax: (701) 777-4257

Ohio

Case Western Reserve University
Mandel School of Applied Social Sciences
10900 Euclid Avenue
Cleveland, OH 44106-7164
Phone: (216) 368-2256
Fax: (216) 368-2850

Ohio State University
College of Social Work
300 Stillman Hall
1947 College Road
Columbus, OH 43210-1162
Phone: (614) 292-2972
Fax: (614) 292-6940

Ohio University
Department of Social Work
Master's Degree Social Work Program
Morton Hall 416
Athens, OH 45701-2979
Phone: (740) 593-1292
Fax: (740) 593-0427

University of Cincinnati
School of Social Work
P.O. Box 210108
Cincinnati, OH 45221-0108
Phone: (513) 556-4615
Fax: (513) 556-2077

Oklahoma

University of Oklahoma
School of Social Work
1005 Jenkins Avenue
Norman, OK 73019
Phone: (405) 325-2821
Fax: (405) 325-7072

Oregon

Portland State University
Graduate School of Social Work
P.O. Box 751
Portland, OR 97207-0751
Phone: (503) 725-4712
Fax: (503) 725-5545

Pennsylvania

Bryn Mawr College
Graduate School of Social Work and Social
Research
300 Airdale Road
Bryn Mawr, PA 19010-1646
Phone: (610) 520-2600
Fax: (610) 520-2655

Temple University
School of Social Administration
1301 Cecil B. Moore Avenue
Ritter Hall Annex, Room 555
Philadelphia, PA 19122
Phone: (215) 204-8623
Fax: (215) 204-9606

University of Pennsylvania
School of Social Policy and Practice
3701 Locust Walk
Philadelphia, PA 19104-6214
Phone: (215) 898-5511
Fax: (215) 573-2099

University of Pittsburgh
School of Social Work
2117 Cathedral of Learning
Pittsburgh, PA 15260
Phone: (412) 624-6304
Fax: (412) 624-6323

Widener University
Center for Social Work Education
One University Place
Chester, PA 19013

Phone: (610) 499-1153
Fax: (610) 499-4617

Puerto Rico

Universidad Interamericana de Puerto Rico,
Recinto Metropolitano
School of Social Work
P.O. Box 191293
San Juan, PR 00919-1293
Phone: (787) 250-1912 x252
Fax: (787) 250-1912

University of Puerto Rico, Rio Piedras Campus
Beatriz Lassalle Graduate School of Social
Work
P.O. Box 23345
San Juan, PR 00931-3345
Phone: (787) 764-0000 x2218
Fax: (787) 772-1482

Rhode Island

Rhode Island College
School of Social Work
Providence, RI 02908
Phone: (401) 456-8042
Fax: (401) 456-8620

South Carolina

University of South Carolina
College of Social Work
Columbia, SC 29208
Phone: (803) 777-5291
Fax: (803) 777-3498

Tennessee

University of Tennessee
College of Social Work
109 Henson Hall

Visit Vault at www.vault.com for insider company profiles, expert advice,
career message boards, expert resume reviews, the Vault Job Board and more.

VAULT CAREER LIBRARY   117

Knoxville, TN 37996-3333
Phone: (865) 974-3176
Fax: (865) 974-4803
Fax (Memphis campus): (901) 448-4850

Texas

Baylor University
School of Social Work
One Bear Place #97320
Waco, TX 76798-7320
Phone: (254) 710-6400
Fax: (254) 710-6455

Stephen F. Austin State University
Master of Social Work Program
School of Social Work
P.O. Box 6104, SFA Station
Nacogdoches, TX 75962-6104
Phone: (936) 468-5105
Fax: (936) 468-7201

University of Houston
Graduate School of Social Work
237 Social Work Building
Houston, TX 77204-4013
Phone: (713) 743-8085
Fax: (713) 743-3267

University of Texas at Austin
School of Social Work
1 University Station D3500
Austin, TX 78712-0358
Phone: (512) 471-1937
Fax: (512) 471-7268

Utah

Brigham Young University
School of Social Work
2190 Joseph F. Smith Building
Provo, UT 84602-4476
Phone: (801) 422-3282
Fax: (801) 422-0624

University of Utah
(1940) (June 2011)
College of Social Work
395 S. 1500 E.
Room 111
Salt Lake City, UT 84112-0260
Phone: (801) 581-6192
Fax: (801) 585-3219

Vermont

University of Vermont
Department of Social Work
443 Waterman Building
85 South Prospect Street
Burlington, VT 05405-0160
Phone: (802) 656-8800
Fax: (802) 656-8565

Virginia

George Mason University
Social Work Program
3330 N. Washington Boulevard
MSN 1F7, Truland Building
Arlington, VA 22201
Phone: (703) 993-4247
Fax: (703) 993-4249

Norfolk State University
Ethelyn R. Strong School of Social Work
700 Park Avenue
Norfolk, VA 23504
Phone: (757) 823-8668
Fax: (757) 823-2556

Virginia Commonwealth University
School of Social Work
1001 W. Franklin Street
P.O. Box 842027
Richmond, VA 23284-2027
Phone: (804) 828-1030
Fax: (804) 828-7541

Washington

University of Washington
School of Social Work
4101 15th Avenue NE
Seattle, WA 98105-6299
Phone: (206) 685-1660
Fax: (206) 221-3910

Walla Walla College
Graduate School of Social Work
204 S. College Avenue
College Place, WA 99324-1198
Phone: (509) 527-2590
Fax: (509) 527-2434

West Virginia

West Virginia University
School of Applied Social Sciences
Division of Social Work
P.O. Box 6830
Morgantown, WV 26506-6830
Phone: (304) 293-3501 x3128
Fax: (304) 293-5936

Wisconsin

University of Wisconsin-Madison
School of Social Work
1350 University Avenue
Madison, WI 53706-1510
Phone: (608) 263-3561
Fax: (608) 263-3836

University of Wisconsin-Milwaukee
Helen Bader School of Social Welfare
Department of Social Work
P.O. Box 786
Milwaukee, WI 53201
Phone: (414) 229-4400
Fax: (414) 229-5311

Wyoming

University of Wyoming
Division of Social Work
1000 University Avenue, Dept. 3632
Laramie, WY 82071
Phone: (307) 766-6112
Fax: (307) 766-6839

Visit Vault at **www.vault.com** for insider company profiles, expert advice,
career message boards, expert resume reviews, the Vault Job Board and more.

VAULT CAREER LIBRARY   **119**

Accredited Baccalaureate Social Work Programs

Alabama

Alabama A&M University
Social Work Department
P.O. Box 302
Normal, AL 35762
Phone: (256) 372-5475
Fax: (256) 372-5484

Alabama State University
Social Work Department
915 S. Jackson Street
P.O. Box 271
Montgomery, AL 36101-0271
Phone: (334) 229-6957
Fax: (334) 229-4962

Talladega College
Social Work Program
627 W. Battle Street
Talladega, AL 35160
Phone: (256) 761-6466
Fax: (256) 761-6342

Tuskegee University
Department of Social Work
Moton Hall 106
Tuskegee, AL 36088
Phone: (334) 727-8300
Fax: (334) 724-4196

University of Alabama
School of Social Work
Box 870314
Tuscaloosa, AL 35487-0314
Phone: (205) 348-3949
Fax: (205) 348-9419

University of Alabama at Birmingham
Department of Anthropology and Social Work
Baccalaureate of Social Work Program
1530 3rd Avenue S.
Birmingham, AL 35294-3350
Phone: (205) 934-3508
Fax: (205) 934-9896

Alaska

University of Alaska Anchorage
School of Social Work
3211 Providence Drive
Anchorage, AK 99508
Phone: (907) 786-6900
Fax: (907) 786-6912

University of Alaska Fairbanks
Department of Social Work
P.O. Box 756480
Fairbanks, AK 99775
Phone: (907) 474-7240
Fax: (907) 474-6085

Arizona

Arizona State University, Tempe Campus
School of Social Work
Box 871802
Tempe, AZ 85287-1802
Phone: (480) 965-2795
Fax: (480) 965-2799

Arizona State University, West Campus
Department of Social Work
College of Human Services--MC: 3251
P.O. Box 37100
Phoenix, AZ 85069-7100
Phone: (602) 543-6602
Fax: (602) 543-6612

Arkansas

Arkansas State University
Social Work Department
P.O. Box 2460
State University, AR 72467
Phone: (870) 972-3984
Fax: (870) 972-3987
E-mail: cjoiner@astate.edu

Harding University
Social Work Program
Department of Behavioral Sciences
900 E. Center Avenue, Box 12260
Searcy, AR 72149-0001
Phone: (501) 279-4561
Fax: (501) 279-4319

Southern Arkansas University
Social Work Program
100 E. University
Magnolia, AR 71753-5000
Phone: (870) 235-4933
Fax: (870) 235-5239

University of Arkansas
School of Social Work
ASUP 106
Fayetteville, AR 72701
Phone: (479) 575-5039
Fax: (479) 575-4145

University of Arkansas at Little Rock
School of Social Work
2801 S. University Avenue
Little Rock, AR 72204
Phone: (501) 569-3046
Fax: (501) 569-3184

University of Arkansas at Pine Bluff
Social Work Program
1200 N. University Drive
Mail Slot 4988
Pine Bluff, AR 71601
Phone: (870) 575-8173
Fax: (870) 543-8920

California

California State University, Fresno
Department of Social Work Education
5310 N. Campus Drive, PH 102
Fresno, CA 93740-8019
Phone: (559) 278-3992
Fax: (559) 278-7191

California State University, Long Beach
Department of Social Work
1250 Bellflower Boulevard
Long Beach, CA 90840-0902
Phone: (562) 985-4204
Fax: (562) 985-5514

California State University, Los Angeles
School of Social Work
5151 State University Drive
Los Angeles, CA 90008
Phone: (323) 343-4680
Fax: (323) 343-6312

California State University, Sacramento
Division of Social Work
6000 J Street
Sacramento, CA 95819-6090
Phone: (916) 278-6943
Fax: (916) 278-7167

San Diego State University
School of Social Work
5500 Campanile Drive
San Diego, CA 92182-4119
Phone: (619) 594-5500
Fax: (619) 594-5991

Visit Vault at www.vault.com for insider company profiles, expert advice,
career message boards, expert resume reviews, the Vault Job Board and more.

VAULT CAREER LIBRARY   121

San Francisco State University
School of Social Work
1600 Holloway Avenue
San Francisco, CA 94132
Phone: (415) 338-1003
Fax: (415) 338-0591

Whittier College
Social Work Program
13406 Philadelphia Street
Whittier, CA 90608
Phone: (562) 907-4804
Fax: (562) 464-4517

Colorado

Colorado State University
School of Social Work
127 Education Building
Fort Collins, CO 80523-1586
Phone: (970) 491-6612
Fax: (970) 491-7280

Metropolitan State College of Denver
Social Work Department
Campus Box 70
P.O. Box 173362
Denver, CO 80217-3362
Phone: (303) 556-4464
Fax: (303) 556-5362

Connecticut

Central Connecticut State University
Social Work Program
1615 Stanley Street
New Britain, CT 06050
Phone: (860) 832-3129
Fax: (860) 832-3130

Eastern Connecticut State University
Social Work Program
83 Windham Street
Willimantic, CT 06226-2295
Phone: (860) 465-4621

Fax: (860) 465-4610

Saint Joseph College
Department of Social Work
1678 Asylum Avenue
West Hartford, CT 06117-2791
Lorrie Greenhouse Gardella, Chair
Phone: (860) 231-5264
Fax: (860) 233-5695
E-mail: lggardella@sjc.edu

Southern Connecticut State University
Department of Social Work
101 Farnham Avenue
New Haven, CT 06515
Phone: (203) 392-6551
Fax: (203) 392-6580

Delaware

Delaware State University
Department of Social Work
Bachelor of Social Work Program
1200 N. DuPont Highway
Dover, DE 19901-2277
Phone: (302) 857-6770
Fax: (302) 857-6794

District of Columbia

Catholic University of America
National Catholic School of Social Service
Baccalaureate Social Work Program
Shahan Hall
Washington, DC 20064
Phone: (202) 319-5479
Fax: (202) 319-5093

Gallaudet University
Department of Social Work
800 Florida Avenue NE
Washington, DC 20002-3695
Phone: (202) 651-5160
Fax: (202) 651-5817

University of the District of Columbia
Social Work Program
4200 Connecticut Avenue NW
Building 41, Room 413
Washington, DC 20008
Phone: (202) 274-7403
Fax: (202) 274-5583

Florida

Florida Agricultural and Mechanical University
Department of Social Work
301 Ware-Rhaney Building
Tallahassee, FL 32307-3500
Phone: (850) 561-2254
Fax: (850) 599-3215

Florida State University
College of Social Work
UCC 2505
Tallahassee, FL 32306-2570
Phone: (850) 644-4751
Fax: (850) 644-9750

University of Central Florida
School of Social Work
P.O. Box 163358
Orlando, FL 32816
Phone: (407) 823-2114
Fax: (407) 823-5697

University of South Florida
School of Social Work
MGY 132
4202 E. Fowler Avenue
Tampa, FL 33620
Phone: (813) 974-0760
Fax: (813) 974-4675

University of West Florida
Division of Social Work
11000 University Parkway
Pensacola, FL 32514-5751
Phone: (850) 474-2375

Fax: (850) 474-2908

Georgia

Albany State University
Social Work Program
Department of Psychology, Sociology and Social Work
504 College Drive
Albany, GA 31705
Phone: (229) 430-4694
Fax: (229) 430-6490

Clark Atlanta University
Whitney M. Young, Jr., School of Social Work
223 James P. Brawley Drive, SW
Atlanta, GA 30314-4391
Phone: (404) 880-8311
Fax: (404) 880-6434

Georgia State University
School of Social Work
College of Health and Human Sciences
MSC 8L0381
33 Gilmer Street, SE Unit 8
Atlanta, GA 30303-3083
Phone: (404) 651-3526
Fax: (404) 651-1863

University of Georgia
School of Social Work
Tucker Hall
Athens, GA 30602-7016
Phone: (706) 542-3364
Fax: (706-542-3282

Idaho

Boise State University
School of Social Work
1910 University Drive
Boise, ID 83725
Phone: (208) 426-1568
Fax: (208) 426-4291

Visit Vault at **www.vault.com** for insider company profiles, expert advice, career message boards, expert resume reviews, the Vault Job Board and more.

VAULT CAREER LIBRARY   **123**

Idaho State University
Department of Sociology, Social Work and
Criminal Justice
Campus Box 8114
Pocatello, ID 83209-8114
Phone: (208) 282-2170
Fax: (208) 282-4733

Lewis-Clark State College
Social Work Program
500 8th Avenue
Lewiston, ID 83501
Phone: (208) 792-2866
Fax: (208) 792-2571

Illinois

Bradley University
Social Work Program
College of Liberal Arts and Sciences
1501 Bradley Avenue
Peoria, IL 61625-0442
Phone: (309) 677-2392
Fax: (309) 677-3872

Governors State University
College of Health Professions
Bachelor of Social Work Program
University Park, IL 60466
Phone: (708) 534-4914
Fax: (708) 235-2196

Illinois State University
School of Social Work
Campus Box 4650
Normal, IL 61790-4650
Phone: (309) 438-3631
Fax: (309) 438-5880

Loyola University of Chicago
School of Social Work
820 N. Michigan Avenue
Chicago, IL 60611
Phone: (312) 915-7005
Fax: (312) 915-7645

Northeastern Illinois University
Social Work Program
5500 N. St. Louis Avenue
Chicago, IL 60625-4699
Phone: (773) 442-4760
Fax: (773) 442-4900

University of Illinois at Chicago
Jane Addams College of Social Work
M/C 309
1040 W. Harrison Street
Chicago, IL 60607
Phone: (312) 996-2204
Fax: (312) 996-2770

University of Illinois at Springfield
Social Work Program
Brookens 338
One University Plaza
Springfield, IL 62703
Phone: (217) 206-6687
Fax: (217) 206-6775

Indiana

Grace College
Social Work Program
200 Seminary Drive
Winona Lake, IN 46590
Phone: (574) 372-5100 x6491
Fax: (574) 372-5139

Indiana State University
Department of Social Work
534 Erickson Hall
Terre Haute, IN 47809
Phone: (812) 237-3611
Fax: (812) 237-8441

Indiana University
School of Social Work
Education Social Work Building
902 W. New York St., ES 4138
Indianapolis, IN 46202-5156
Phone: (317) 274-6725

Fax: (317) 274-8630

Branch Indiana University:
Bloomington Campus
School of Social Work
1127 Atwater Avenue
Bloomington, IN 47405
Phone: (812) 855-4427
Fax: (812) 855-6110

Branch
Indiana University: East Campus
School of Social Work
Middle Fork Hall 264
2325 Chester Boulevard
Richmond, IN 47374
Phone: (765) 973-8422
Fax: (765) 973-8508

Indiana Wesleyan University
Department of Social Work
4201 S. Washington Street
Marion, IN 46953
Phone: (765) 677-2263
Fax: (765) 677-2487

Saint Mary's College
Social Work Program
131 Madeleva Hall
Notre Dame, IN 46556-5001
Phone: (574) 284-4515
Fax: (574) 284-4716

Taylor University
Social Work Department
236 W. Reade Avenue
Upland, IN 46989-1001
Phone: (765) 998-5353
Fax: (765) 998-4980

University of Indianapolis
Phylis Lan Lin Program in Social Work
1400 East Hanna Avenue
Indianapolis, IN 46227-3697
Phone: (317) 788-3535

Fax: (317) 788-3480

University of Saint Francis
Department of Social Work
2701 Spring Street
Fort Wayne, IN 46808
Phone: (260) 434-7436
Fax: (260) 434-7562

University of Southern Indiana
Social Work Department
8600 University Boulevard
Evansville, IN 47712
Phone: (812) 464-1843
Fax: (812) 465-1116

Iowa

Briar Cliff University
Department of Social Work
Box 2100
3303 Rebecca Street
Sioux City, IA 51104-0100
Phone: (712) 279-5321 x5489
Fax: (712) 279-5410

Clarke College
Bi-College Social Work Program
1550 Clarke Drive
Social Work Department
Dubuque, IA 52001
Phone: (563) 588-6368
Fax: (563) 584-8604

Mount Mercy College
Department of Social Work
1330 Elmhurst Drive NE
Cedar Rapids, IA 52402
Phone: (319) 363-8213 x1384
Fax: (319) 363-5270

Northwestern College
Social Work Department
101 7th Street SW
Orange City, IA 51041

Visit Vault at **www.vault.com** for insider company profiles, expert advice,
career message boards, expert resume reviews, the Vault Job Board and more.

VAULT CAREER LIBRARY   **125**

Phone: (712) 707-7085
Fax: (712) 707-7247

University of Iowa
School of Social Work
308 North Hall
Iowa City, IA 5242-1223
Phone: (319) 335-1250
Fax: (319) 335-1711

University of Northern Iowa
Department of Social Work
30 Sabin Hall
Cedar Falls, IA 50614-0405
Phone: (319) 273-6249
Fax: (319) 273-6976

Kansas

Bethany College
Social Work Program
Lindsborg, KS 67456
Phone: (785) 227-3380 x8171

Kansas State University
Department of Sociology, Anthropology and
Social Work
204 Waters Hall
Manhattan, KS 66506
Phone: (785) 532-4980
Fax: (785) 532-6978

Pittsburg State University
Social Work Program
Social Science Department
1701 South Broadway, Russ Hall
Pittsburg, KS 66762
Phone: (620) 235-4331
Fax: (620) 235-4080

University of Kansas
School of Social Welfare
1545 Lilac Lane
Lawrence, KS 66044-3184

Phone: (785) 864-8968
Fax: (785) 864-5277

Wichita State University
School of Social Work
Box 154
1845 Fairmount
Wichita, KS 67260-0154
Phone: (316) 978-7250
Fax: (316) 978-3328

Kentucky

Asbury College
Social Work Program
Sociology and Social Work
1 Macklem Drive
Wilmore, KY 40390
Phone: (859) 858-3511 x2210
Fax: (859) 858-3921

Campbellsville University
Carver School of Social Work
1 University Drive
Campbellsville, KY 42718-2799
Phone: (270) 789-5049
Fax: (270) 789-5542

Kentucky State University
Social Work Program
Division of Social Work and Criminal Justice
Hathaway Hall 220
Frankfort, KY 40601
Phone: (502) 597-6890
Fax: (502) 597-6715

Morehead State University
Social Work Program
Radar Hall
Morehead, KY 40351
Phone: (606) 783-2263
Fax: (606) 783-5070

Spalding University
School of Social Work
851 S. Fourth Street
Louisville, KY 40202-2188
Phone: (502) 585-9911 x2183
Fax: (502) 992-2413

University of Kentucky
College of Social Work
619 Patterson Office Tower
Lexington, KY 40506-0027
Phone: (859) 257-4407
Fax: (859) 323-1030

Western Kentucky University
Department of Social Work
AC 211
1 Big Red Way
Bowling Green, KY 42101
Phone: (270) 745-2693
Fax: (270) 745-6841

Louisiana

Grambling State University
School of Social Work
P.O. Box 907
Grambling, LA 71245
Phone: (318) 274-3166
Fax: (318) 274-3254

Louisiana College
Social Work Program
P.O. Box 605
Pineville, LA 71359
Phone: (318) 487-7115
Fax: (318) 487-7516

Northwestern State University of Louisiana
Department of Social Work
Natchitoches, LA 71497
Phone: (318) 357-5493
Fax: (318) 357-6782

Southeastern Louisiana University
Social Work Program
SLU 686
Hammond, LA 70402
Phone: (985) 549-2080
Fax: (985) 549-2080

Southern University and A & M College
Department of Social Work
Suite 306, R.G. Higgins Hall
Southern University Branch, P.O. Box 9243
Baton Rouge, LA 70813-2042
Phone: (225) 771-5450
Fax: (225) 771-4234

Southern University at New Orleans
School of Social Work
6400 Press Drive
New Orleans, LA 70126
Phone: (504) 286-5376
Fax: (504) 286-5387

Maine

University of Maine
School of Social Work
5570 Social Work Building
Orono, ME 04469-5770
Diane C. Haslett, Coordinator
Phone: (207) 581-2389
Fax: (207) 581-2396

University of Southern Maine
Department of Social Work
96 Falmouth Street
P.O. Box 9300
Portland, ME 04104-9300
Phone: (207) 780-4120
Fax: (207) 780-4902

Visit Vault at **www.vault.com** for insider company profiles, expert advice,
career message boards, expert resume reviews, the Vault Job Board and more.

V/\ULT CAREER LIBRARY   **127**

Maryland

Morgan State University
Department of Social Work
Jenkins Building, Room 422
1700 Cold Spring Lane
Baltimore, MD 21251
Phone: (443) 885-3537
Fax: (443) 885-8241

Salisbury University
Department of Social Work
1101 Camden Avenue
Salisbury, MD 21801
Phone: (410) 543-6305
Fax: (410) 548-2593

University of Maryland-Baltimore County
Department of Social Work
Academic IV Building, Wing B, Room 322
1000 Hilltop Circle
Baltimore, MD 21250
Phone: (410) 455-2144
Fax: (410) 455-2974

Massachusetts

Eastern Nazarene College
Department of Social Work
23 E. Elm Avenue
Quincy, MA 02170
Phone: (617) 745-3565
Fax: (617) 745-3939

Salem State College
School of Social Work
352 Lafayette Street
Salem, MA 01970
Phone: (978) 542-6629
Fax: (978) 542-6936

Western New England College
Department of Social Work
1215 Wilbraham Road
Springfield, MA 01119
Phone: (413) 782-1756
Fax: (413) 796-2118

Westfield State College
Department of Sociology and Social Work
Westfield, MA 01086-1630
Phone: (413) 572-5536
Fax: (413) 562-3613

Michigan

Andrews University
Social Work Department
Nethery Hall
Berrien Springs, MI 49104-0038
Phone: (269) 471-6249
Fax: (269) 471-3686

Central Michigan University
Social Work Program
Department of Sociology, Anthropology and
Social Work
34 Anspach Hall
Mount Pleasant, MI 48859
Phone: (989) 774-2690
Fax: (989) 774-2140

Eastern Michigan University
BSW Program Office
303 Marshall Building
Ypsilanti, MI 48197
Phone: (734) 487-6807
Fax: (734) 487-6832

Grand Valley State University
School of Social Work
3rd Floor, DeVos Center
401 W. Fulton Street
Grand Rapids, MI 49504
Phone: (616) 331-6550
Fax: (616) 331-6570

Hope College
Social Work Program
Holland, MI 49422-9000
Phone: (616) 395-7553
Fax: (616) 395-7617

Michigan State University
School of Social Work
254 Baker Hall
East Lansing, MI 48824
Phone: (517) 432-3728
Fax: (517) 353-3038

Northern Michigan University
Social Work Program
Department of Sociology and Social Work
Marquette, MI 49855
Phone: (906) 227-2706
Fax: (906) 227-1212

University of Michigan-Flint
Social Work Program
303 E. Kearsley Street
Flint, MI 48502-2186
Phone: (810) 762-3390
Fax: (810) 237-6541

Wayne State University
School of Social Work
Thompson Home
4756 Cass Avenue
Detroit, MI 48202
Phone: (313) 577-4433
Fax: (313) 577-8770

Western Michigan University
School of Social Work
1903 West Michigan Avenue
Kalamazoo, MI 49008-5354
Phone: (269) 387-3180
Fax: (269) 387-3183

Minnesota

Bethel University
Social Work Program
3900 Bethel Drive
St Paul, MN 55112-6999
Phone: (651) 638-6037
Fax: (651) 638-6001

Metropolitan State University
Social Work Program
700 E. 7th Street
St. Paul, MN 55106
Phone: (651) 793-1339
Fax: (651) 793-1355

Minnesota State University Moorhead
Social Work Department
Lommen Hall 83
1104 7th Avenue S.
Moorhead, MN 56563
Phone: (218) 477-2615
Fax: (218) 236-3642

Saint John's University
(In collaboration with College of Saint Benedict)
Department of Social Work
37 South College Avenue
St. Joseph, MN 56374-2099
Phone: (320) 363-5155
Fax: (320) 363-6103

Southwest Minnesota State University
Social Work Program
Social Sciences Building 103B
1501 State Street
Marshall, MN 56258
Phone: (507) 537-7336
Fax: (507) 537-6115

Visit Vault at **www.vault.com** for insider company profiles, expert advice, career message boards, expert resume reviews, the Vault Job Board and more.

VAULT CAREER LIBRARY   **129**

St. Olaf College
Social Work Program
1520 St. Olaf Avenue
Northfield, MN 55057-1098
Phone: (507) 646-3945
Fax: (507) 646-3896

Winona State University
Social Work Program
Minne Hall 228
Winona, MN 55987
Phone: (507) 457-5420
Fax: (507) 457-5086

Mississippi

Delta State University
Department of Social Work
P.O. Box 3172
Cleveland, MS 38733
Phone: (662) 846-4407
Fax: (662) 846-4403

University of Mississippi
Department of Social Work
208 Hume Hall
P.O. Box 1848
University, MS 38677-1848
Phone: (662) 915-7336
Fax: (662) 915-1288

University of Southern Mississippi
School of Social Work
Box 5114
Hattiesburg, MS 39406
Phone: (601) 266-4163
Fax: (601) 266-4165

Missouri

Avila University
School of Science and Social Work
Social Work Program
11901 Wornall Road
Kansas City, MO 64145

Phone: (816) 501-3647
Fax: (816) 501-2457

Central Missouri State University
Social Work Program
Department of Sociology and Social Work
Wood Hall 203
Warrensburg, MO 64093
Phone: (660) 543-8716
Fax: (660) 543-8215

Missouri State University
School of Social Work
Professional Building, Suite 200
901 S. National Avenue
Springfield, MO 65804-0095
Phone: (417) 836-6953
Fax: (417) 836-7688

Saint Louis University
School of Social Work
3550 Lindell Boulevard
St. Louis, MO 63103
Phone: (314) 977-2712
Fax: (314) 977-2731

University of Missouri-Columbia
School of Social Work
729 Clark Hall
Columbia, MO 65211-4470
Phone: (573) 884-9385
Fax: (573) 882-8926

University of Missouri-St. Louis
School of Social Welfare
College of Arts and Sciences
One University Boulevard
St. Louis, MO 63121-4400
Phone: (314) 516-6385
Fax: (314) 516-5816

Montana

University of Montana
School of Social Work
Jeanette Rankin Hall
Missoula, MT 59812
Phone: (406) 243-5543
Fax: (406) 243-5275

Nebraska

Chadron State College
Social Work Program
1000 Main St.
Chadron, NE 69337
Phone: (800) 242-3766

Creighton University
Department of Social Work
Administration 437
2500 California Plaza
Omaha, NE 68178
Phone: (402) 280-2079
Fax: (402) 280-2108

Union College
Social Work Program
3800 S. 48th Street
Lincoln, NE 68506
Phone: (402) 486-2522 x2174

Nevada

University of Nevada, Las Vegas
School of Social Work
4505 Maryland Parkway
P.O. Box 455032
Las Vegas, NV 89154-5032
Phone: (702) 895-3311
Fax: (702) 895-4079

University of Nevada, Reno
School of Social Work
Amsari Business Building, Room 523
Mail Stop 090

Reno, NV 89557-0068
Phone: (775) 784-6542
Fax: (775) 784-4573

New Hampshire

Plymouth State University
Department of Social Work
MSC #57
17 High Street
Plymouth, NH 03264
Phone: (603) 535-2703
Fax: (603) 535-2854

University of New Hampshire
Department of Social Work
Pettee Hall
55 College Road
Durham, NH 03824-3596
Phone: (603) 862-1799
Fax: (603) 862-4374

New Jersey

Kean University
Bachelor of Social Work Program
1000 Morris Avenue
Union, NJ 07083-7131
Phone: (908) 737-4030
Fax: (908) 737-4064

Monmouth University
Department of Social Work
400 Cedar Avenue
West Long Branch, NJ 07764
Phone: (732) 571-3543
Fax: (732) 263-5217

Ramapo College
Social Work Program
505 Ramapo Valley Road
Mahwah, NJ 07430-1680
Phone: (201) 684-7649
Fax: (201) 684-7257

Visit Vault at **www.vault.com** for insider company profiles, expert advice,
career message boards, expert resume reviews, the Vault Job Board and more.

V/\ULT CAREER LIBRARY   **131**

Richard Stockton College of New Jersey
Social Work Program
Social and Behavioral Sciences Division
Jim Leeds Road, P.O. Box 195
Pomona, NJ 08240
Phone: (609) 652-4512
Fax: (609) 748-5559

Rutgers, The State University of New Jersey
School of Social Work
536 George Street
New Brunswick, NJ 08901-1167
Phone: (732) 932-7011
Fax: (732) 932-8181

Seton Hall University
Department of Social Work
400 S. Orange Avenue
Arts and Sciences Hall, Room 104
South Orange, NJ 07079
Phone: (973) 761-9470
Fax: (973) 275-2366

New Mexico

New Mexico State University
School of Social Work
P.O. Box 30001
MSC 3SW
Las Cruces, NM 88003-8001
Phone: (505) 646-2143
Fax: (505) 646-4116

New York

Adelphi University
School of Social Work
South Avenue
Garden City, NY 11530
Phone: (516) 877-4362
Fax: (516) 877-4392

Buffalo State College
Social Work Department

1300 Elmwood Avenue
Buffalo, NY 14222
Phone: (716) 878-5705
Fax: (716) 878-3240

College of New Rochelle
Social Work Department
29 Castle Place
New Rochelle, NY 10805-2339
Phone: (914) 654-5392
Fax: (914) 654-5259

College of Saint Rose
Social Work Department
432 Western Avenue
Albany, NY 12203
Phone: (518) 454-5234
Fax: (518) 458-5446

Concordia College
Social Work Program
171 White Plains Road
Bronxville, NY 10708
Phone: (914) 337-9300 x2178
Fax: (914) 395-4500

Fordham University
Baccalaureate Program in Social Work
113 W. 60th Street
New York, NY 10023-7479
Phone: (212) 636-6668
Fax: (212) 636-7876

Iona College
Social Work Department
715 North Avenue
New Rochelle, NY 10801
Phone: (914) 633-2471
Fax: (914) 637-7743

Lehman College, City University of New York
Department of Sociology and Social Work
250 Bedford Park Boulevard West
Bronx, NY 10468-1589

Phone: (718) 960-8418
Fax: (718) 960-7402

Long Island University-C.W. Post
Social Work Department
Post Hall 1E8
720 Northern Boulevard
Brookville, NY 11548
Phone: (516) 299-3924
Fax: (516) 299-3911

Marist College
Social Work Program
Poughkeepsie, NY 12601-1387
Phone: (845) 575-3000 x2970
Fax: (845) 575-3965

Mercy College
Social Work Program
555 Broadway
Dobbs Ferry, NY 10522
Phone: (914) 674-7439
Fax: (914) 674-7413

Nazareth College of Rochester
Social Work Department
4245 East Avenue
Rochester, NY 14618-3790
Phone: (585) 389-2753
Fax: (585) 389-2757

New York University
School of Social Work
1 Washington Square North
New York, NY 10003
Phone: (212) 998-5944
Fax: (212) 995-4172

Roberts Wesleyan College
Division of Social Work
BSW Program
2301 Westside Drive
Rochester, NY 14624-1997
Phone: (585) 594-6410
Fax: (585) 594-6480

Siena College
Social Work Department
Social Work House
515 Loudon Road
Loudonville, NY 12211-1462
Phone: (518) 786-5046
Fax: (518) 782-6499

Skidmore College
Social Work Program
815 N. Broadway
Saratoga Springs, NY 12866
Phone: (518) 580-5428
Fax: (518) 580-5429

State University of New York at Stony Brook
School of Social Welfare
Health Sciences Center
Level 2, Room 093
Stony Brook, NY 11794-8231
Phone: (631) 444-3165
Fax: (631) 444-7565

State University of New York, College at Brockport
Social Work Department
170 Faculty Office Building
350 New Campus Drive
Brockport, NY 14420
Phone: (585) 395-2324
Fax: (585) 395-2366

Syracuse University
School of Social Work
Sims Hall
Syracuse, NY 13244-1230
Phone: (315) 443-4252
Fax: (315) 443-5576

University at Albany, State University of New York
School of Social Welfare
135 Western Avenue
Albany, NY 12222

Visit Vault at www.vault.com for insider company profiles, expert advice,
career message boards, expert resume reviews, the Vault Job Board and more.

VAULT CAREER LIBRARY   **133**

Phone: (518) 442-5340
Fax: (518) 442-5380

York College of the City University of New York
Social Work Program
94-20 Guy R. Brewer Boulevard
Jamaica, NY 11451
Phone: (718) 262-2605
Fax: (718) 262-3790

North Carolina

Bennett College
Social Work Program
Black Hall, Suite 200
900 E. Washington Street
Greensboro, NC 27401-3239
Phone: (336) 517-2177
Fax: (336) 517-2184

Methodist College
Social Work Program
5400 Ramsey Street
Fayetteville, NC 28311-1420
Phone: (910) 630-7059 x7059
Fax: (910) 630-7679

North Carolina A&T State University
Department of Sociology and Social Work
201 Gibbs Social Science Building
1601 E. Market Street
Greensboro, NC 27411-0002
Phone: (336) 334-7895
Fax: (336) 334-7197

North Carolina State University
Department of Social Work
Box 7639
1911 Building, Room 231
Raleigh, NC 27695-7639
Phone: (919) 515-2492
Fax: (919) 515-4403

University of North Carolina at Charlotte
Bachelor of Social Work Program
Department of Social Work
9201 University City Boulevard
Charlotte, NC 28223-0001
Phone: (704) 687-4076
Fax: (704) 687-2343

University of North Carolina at Greensboro
Department of Social Work
P.O. Box 26170
Greensboro, NC 27402-6170
Phone: (336) 334-5147
Fax: (336) 334-5210

Western Carolina University
Department of Social Work
G02 McKee
Cullowhee, NC 28723
Phone: (828) 227-7112
Fax: (828) 227-7061

North Dakota

University of North Dakota
Department of Social Work
Gillette Hall
P.O. Box 7135
Grand Forks, ND 58202-7135
Phone: (701) 777-2669
Fax: (701) 777-4257

Ohio

Ashland University
Department of Social Work
401 College Avenue
Ashland, OH 44805
Phone: (419) 289-5344
Fax: (419) 289-5665

Bowling Green State University
Social Work Program
Health Center Building
Bowling Green, OH 43403-0284
Phone: (419) 372-2326
Fax: (419) 372-2400

Cleveland State University
Social Work Program
2121 Euclid Avenue
Cleveland, OH 44115
Phone: (216) 687-4599
Fax: (216) 687-5590

Ohio State University
Baccalaureate Social Work Program
College of Social Work
1947 College Road, 308 Stillman Hall
Columbus, OH 43210
Phone: (614) 292-7488
Fax: (614) 292-6940

Ohio University
Department of Social Work
416 Morton Hall
Athens, OH 45701
Phone: (740) 593-1292
Fax: (740) 593-0427

University of Akron
School of Social Work
Polsky Building, Room 411
Akron, OH 44325-8001
Phone: (330) 972-5275
Fax: (330) 972-5739

University of Cincinnati
School of Social Work
P.O. Box 210108
Cincinnati, OH 45221-0108
Phone: (513) 556-4615
Fax: (513) 556-2077

University of Toledo
Social Work Department, MS 119
College of Health and Human Services
2801 W. Bancroft Street
Toledo, OH 43607
Phone: (419) 530-4140
Fax: (419) 530-4141

Wright State University
Social Work Department
270 Millett Hall
Dayton, OH 45435
Phone: (937) 775-2751
Fax: (937) 775-4228

Xavier University
Social Work Department
3800 Victory Parkway
Cincinnati, OH 45207-7372
Phone: (513) 745-4262
Fax: (513) 745-3220

Youngstown State University
Social Work Department
Cushwa Hall, Room 3030
Youngstown, OH 44555
Phone: (330) 941-1598
Fax: (330) 941-3774

Oklahoma

Northeastern State University
Social Work Program
College of Liberal Arts
Department of Social and Professional Services
Tahlequah, OK 74464-2302
Phone: (918) 456-5511 x3511
Fax: (918) 458-2346

Oral Roberts University
Social Work Program
7777 S. Lewis Ave.
Tulsa, OK 74171
Phone: (918) 495-6543

Visit Vault at **www.vault.com** for insider company profiles, expert advice,
career message boards, expert resume reviews, the Vault Job Board and more.

V/\ULT CAREER LIBRARY   **135**

Fax: (918) 495-6011

Southwestern Oklahoma State University
Social Work Program
100 Campus Drive
Weatherford, OK 73096-3098
Phone: (580) 774-3154
Fax: (580) 774-3795

University of Oklahoma
School of Social Work
1005 Jenkins Avenue
Norman, OK 73019-0475
Phone: (405) 325-2821
Fax: (405) 325-7072

Oregon

George Fox University
Social Work Program
414 N Meridian Street
Newberg, OR 97132-2697
Phone: (503) 554-2740
Fax: (503) 537-3886

Pennsylvania
Cabrini College
Social Work Program
610 King of Prussia Road
Radnor, PA 19087-3698
Phone: (610) 902-8357
Fax: (610) 902-8285

Eastern University
Social Work Department
1300 Eagle Road
St. Davids, PA 19087-3696
Phone: (610) 341-5878
Fax: (610) 341-1460

La Salle University
Department of Sociology, Social Work and Criminal Justice
Social Work Program

1900 W. Olney Avenue
Philadelphia, PA 19141-1199
Phone: (215) 951-1119
Fax: (215) 951-1488

Saint Francis University
Social Work Program
309 Scotus
Loretto, PA 15940
Phone: (814) 472-3344
Fax: (814) 472-2787

Seton Hill University
Social Work Program
Seton Hill Drive
Greensburg, PA 15601
Phone: (724) 830-1065 x4542
Fax: (724) 724-1295

Temple University
School of Social Administration
Ritter Annex, Room 555
1301 Cecil B. Moore Avenue
Philadelphia, PA 19122
Phone: (215) 204-5923
Fax: (215) 204-9606

University of Pittsburgh
School of Social Work
2117 Cathedral of Learning
Pittsburgh, PA 15260
Phone: (412) 624-6304
Fax: (412) 624-6323

West Chester University
Undergraduate Social Work Department
114 Rosedale Avenue
West Chester, PA 19383
Phone: (610) 436-2527
Fax: (610) 436-2135

Widener University
Center for Social Work Education
One University Place
Chester, PA 19013

Richard Cooper, Director
Phone: (610) 499-1153
Fax: (610) 499-4617

Rhode Island

Providence College
Department of Social Work
Howley Hall
Providence, RI 02918-0001
Phone: (401) 865-2526
Fax: (401) 865-2232

Rhode Island College
School of Social Work
Providence, RI 02908
Phone: (401) 456-8171
Fax: (401) 456-8620

South Carolina

Benedict College
Social Work Department
1600 Harden Street
Columbia, SC 29204
Phone: (803) 253-5345
Fax: (803) 758-4490

Columbia College
Social Work Program
Department of Human Relations
1301 Columbia College Drive
Columbia, SC 29203
Phone: (803) 786-3687
Fax: (803) 786-3790

South Carolina State University
Social Work Program
Department of Human Services
300 College St. NE, P.O. Box 7595
Orangeburg, SC 29117
Phone: (803) 533-3609
Fax: (803) 533-3666

Winthrop University
Department of Social Work
Rock Hill, SC 29733
Phone: (803) 323-2168
Fax: (803) 323-2176

South Dakota

University of Sioux Falls
Social Work Program
1101 West 22nd Street
Sioux Falls, SD 57105-1699
Phone: (605) 331-6766

University of South Dakota
Social Work Program
414 E. Clark Street
Vermillion, SD 57069
Phone: (605) 677-5401
Fax: (605) 677-5583

Tennessee

Austin Peay State University
Department of Social Work and Sociology
Box 4656
Clarksville, TN 37044
Phone: (931) 221-7728
Fax: (931) 221-6440

East Tennessee State University
Department of Social Work
P.O. Box 70645
Johnson City, TN 37614-1702
Phone: (423) 439-4372
Fax: (423) 439-4471

Lincoln Memorial University
Social Work Program
Harrogate, TN 37752-0901
Phone: (423) 869-6323
Fax: (423) 869-6455

Visit Vault at **www.vault.com** for insider company profiles, expert advice,
career message boards, expert resume reviews, the Vault Job Board and more.

VAULT CAREER LIBRARY   **137**

Middle Tennessee State University
Social Work Department
P.O. Box 139
Murfreesboro, TN 37132
Phone: (615) 898-2868
Fax: (615) 898-5428

Tennessee State University
Department of Social Work and Sociology
P.O. Box 9525
3500 John Merritt Boulevard
Nashville, TN 37209-1561
Phone: (615) 963-7641
Fax: (615) 963-7672

University of Memphis
Division of Social Work
School of Urban Affairs and Public Policy
McCord Hall 119
Memphis, TN 38152
Phone: (901) 678-2616
Fax: (901) 678-2981

University of Tennessee, Knoxville
College of Social Work
303 Henson Hall
Knoxville, TN 37996-3333
Phone: (865) 974-3352
Fax: (865) 974-3701

Texas

Baylor University
School of Social Work
One Bear Place #97320
Waco, TX 76798-7320
Phone: (254) 710-6400
Fax: (254) 710-6455

Howard Payne University
Social Work Program
1000 Fisk Avenue
Brownwood, TX 76801
Phone: (915) 646-2502
Fax: (915) 649-8928

Lamar University
Social Work Program
Department of Sociology, Social Work and
Criminal Justice
P.O. Box 10026
Beaumont, TX 77710
Phone: (490) 880-8552
Fax: (409) 880-2324

Midwestern State University
Social Work Program
3410 Taft Boulevard
Wichita Falls, TX 76308
Phone: (940) 397-4437
Fax: (940) 397-6291

St. Edward's University
Social Work Program
3001 S. Congress Avenue
Austin, TX 78704
Phone: (512) 448-8642
Fax: (512) 448-8492

Tarleton State University
Department of Social Work, Sociology and
Criminal Justice
Box T 0665
Stephenville, TX 76402
Phone: (254) 968-9276
Fax: (254) 968-9288

Texas A&M International University
Department of Psychology, Sociology and
Social Work
Social Work Program
5201 University Boulevard
Laredo, TX 78041-1900
Phone: (956) 326-2644
Fax: (956) 326-2474

Texas Southern University
Department of Social Work
3100 Cleburne
Houston, TX 77004
Phone: (713) 313-7425

Fax: (713) 313-1960

Texas Tech University
Social Work Division
Department of Sociology, Anthropology
and Social Work
P.O. Box 41012
Lubbock, TX 79409-1012
Phone: (806) 742-2401 x244
Fax: (806) 742-1088

Texas Woman's University
Social Work Program
Department of Sociology and Social Work
P.O. Box 425887
Denton, TX 76204
Phone: (940) 898-2071
Fax: (940) 898-2068

University of Mary Hardin-Baylor
Social Work Program
UMHB Box 8014
900 College Street
Belton, TX 76513
Phone: (254) 295-4554
Fax: (254) 295-4535

University of North Texas
Social Work Program
Department of Rehabilitation, Social Work
and Addictions
P.O. Box 311456
Denton, TX 76203-1456
Phone: (940) 565-2488
Fax: (940) 565-3960

University of Texas at Austin
School of Social Work
1 University Station D3500
Austin, TX 78712
Phone: (512) 471-5457
Fax: (512) 471-9600

West Texas A&M University
Social Work Program
WTAMU Box 60296
University Station
Canyon, TX 79016
Phone: (806) 651-2592
Fax: (806) 651-2728

Utah

Brigham Young University
School of Social Work
2190 Joseph F. Smith Building
Provo, UT 84602-4476
Phone: (801) 422-3282
Fax: (801) 422-0624

University of Utah
College of Social Work
395 S. 1500 E.
Room 111
Salt Lake City, UT 84112-0260
Phone: (801) 581-6192
Fax: (801) 585-3219

Utah State University
Department of Sociology, Social Work and
Anthropology
Social Work Program
UMC 0730
Logan, UT 84322
Phone: (435) 797-4080
Fax: (435) 797-1240

Weber State University
Department of Social Work and
Gerontology
1211 University Circle
Ogden, UT 84408-1211
Phone: (801) 626-6155
Fax: (801) 626-8070

Visit Vault at **www.vault.com** for insider company profiles, expert advice,
career message boards, expert resume reviews, the Vault Job Board and more.

VAULT CAREER LIBRARY   **139**

Vermont

University of Vermont
Department of Social Work
443 Waterman Building
Burlington, VT 05405-0160
Phone: (802) 656-8800
Fax: (802) 656-8565

Virginia

Eastern Mennonite University
Social Work Program
1200 Park Road
Harrisonburg, VA 22802-2462
Phone: (540) 432-4450
Fax: (540) 432-4449

George Mason University
Social Work Department
4400 University Drive
MSN 1F8-Robinson Hall B378
Fairfax, VA 22030
Phone: (703) 993-2030
Fax: (703) 993-2889

James Madison University
Department of Social Work
MSC 4303
Harrisonburg, VA 22807
Phone: (540) 568-6980
Fax: (540) 568-7896

Norfolk State University
Ethelyn R. Strong School of Social Work
700 Park Avenue
Norfolk, VA 23504
Phone: (757) 823-8668
Fax: (757) 823-2556

Radford University
School of Social Work
Box 6958
Radford, VA 24142
Phone: (540) 831-7689
Fax: (540) 831-7670

Virginia Commonwealth University
School of Social Work
1001 W. Franklin Street
P.O. Box 842027
Richmond, VA 23284-2027
Phone: (804) 828-0703
Fax: (804) 828-0716

Virginia Union University
Social Work Department
1500 N. Lombardy Street
Richmond, VA 23220
Phone: (804) 257-5770
Fax: (804) 257-5774

Washington

Eastern Washington University
School of Social Work and Human Services
203 Senior Hall
Cheney, WA 99004-2441
Phone: (509) 359-2282
Fax: (509) 359-6475

Heritage College
Social Work Program
Division of Human Services
3240 Fort Road
Toppenish, WA 98948
Phone: (509) 865-8500 x3721
Fax: (509) 865-4469

Pacific Lutheran University
Social Work Program
Department of Sociology and Social Work
Tacoma, WA 98447
Phone: (253) 535-7294
Fax: (253) 535-8305

Seattle University
Department of Social Work
900 Broadway
Seattle, WA 98122-4340
Phone: (206) 296-5906
Fax: (206) 296-5997

University of Washington
School of Social Work
4101 15th Avenue NE
Seattle, WA 98105-6299
Phone: (206) 685-1660
Fax: (206) 221-3910

Walla Walla College
School of Social Work and Sociology
204 S. College Avenue
College Place, WA 99324
Phone: (509) 527-2273 x2410
Fax: (509) 527-2270

West Virginia

Bethany College
Social Work Program
Steinman Hall
Bethany, WV 26032
Phone: (304) 829-7189
Fax: (304) 829-7192

Concord University
Social Work Program
Athens, WV 24712
Phone: (304) 384-5218
Fax: (304) 384-6091

Marshall University
Social Work Department
1 John Marshall Drive
Old Main 307
Huntington, WV 25755-9465
Phone: (304) 696-2792
Fax: (304) 696-6431

West Virginia State University
Social Work Department
Wallace Hall 927
P.O. Box 1000
Institute, WV 25112-1000
Phone: (304) 766-3307 x3307
Fax: (304) 766-3272

West Virginia University
Division of Social Work
School of Applied Social Sciences
P.O. Box 6830
Morgantown, WV 26506
Phone: (304) 293-3501 x3128
Fax: (304) 293-5936

Wisconsin

Carthage College
Department of Social Work
2001 Alford Drive
Kenosha, WI 53140-1994
Phone: (262) 551-5829
Fax: (262) 551-6208

Concordia University Wisconsin
Social Work Department
KA 115
12800 N. Lake Shore Drive
Mequon, WI 53097-2402
Phone: (262) 243-4272
Fax: (262) 243-4453

Visit Vault at www.vault.com for insider company profiles, expert advice,
career message boards, expert resume reviews, the Vault Job Board and more.

VAULT CAREER LIBRARY   141

Marian College of Fond du Lac
Social Work Program
45 S. National Avenue
Fond du Lac, WI 54935-4699
Phone: (920) 923-8733
Fax: (920) 923-8098

Mount Mary College
Social Work Program
2900 N. Menomonee River Parkway
Milwaukee, WI 53222-4597
Phone: (414) 256-1229
Fax: (414) 256-1224

University of Wisconsin-Eau Claire
Department of Social Work
Eau Claire, WI 54702-4004
Phone: (715) 836-4466
Fax: (715) 836-5077

University of Wisconsin-Green Bay
Social Work Professional Program
Room CL710
2420 Nicolet Drive
Green Bay, WI 54311
Phone: (920) 465-2567
Fax: (920) 465-2824

University of Wisconsin-Madison
School of Social Work
1350 University Avenue
Madison, WI 53706-1510
Phone: (608) 263-3660
Fax: (608) 263-3836

University of Wisconsin-Milwaukee
Helen Bader School of Social Welfare
P.O. Box 786
Milwaukee, WI 53201
Phone: (414) 229-4400
Fax: (414) 229-5311

University of Wisconsin-Oshkosh
Department of Social Work
800 Algoma Boulevard
Oshkosh, WI 54901-8672
Phone: (920) 424-1419
Fax: (920) 424-1443

Wyoming

University of Wyoming
Division of Social Work
100 University Avenue
Dept. 3632
Laramie, WY 82071
Phone: (307) 766-6112
Fax: (307) 766-6839

Financial Aid Resources

Helpful Web Sites

www.fafsa.ed.gov — universal application for federal loans and grants

www.fastweb.com — searchable database of private scholarships

www.fie.com/molis — Minority On-Line Information Service

www.collegeboard.org/fundfinder/bin/fundfind01.p1 — The College Board

www.finaid.org — The Financial Aid Information Page

www.ed.gov — U.S Department of Education

Scholarships and Awards

American Board of Examiners in Clinical Social Work
ABE Students Awards Program.
27 Congress St. #211
Salem, MA 01970
Phone: (800) 694-5285
Fax: (800) 694-7882
http://www.abecsw.org

The awards recognize excellence in student professional development demonstrated by original clinical practice papers. The paper must be an original, excellent work written by a second-year social work master's degree candidate and based on the candidate's clinical work in his/her placement setting.

Baker Foundation
c/o Windels, Marx, Davies & Ives
156 West 56th Street
New York, NY 10019

For students who have been unable to obtain funding from other sources such as student loans, scholarships, etc. Applicants must show that they have applied for such funding and been turned down.

Board of Education Program of the City of New York
Division of Human Resources
Loan Forgiveness Program
Bureau of Recruitment Programs, Room 101
65 Court Street Brooklyn, NY 11201
Att: Mrs. Pamela Conroy

Will repay student loans to eligible applicants in exchange for their
employment in shortage area positions. To qualify students must meet
eligibility requirements.

Hattie M. Strong Foundation
1620 Eye Street, NW, Suite 700
Washington, DC 20006
Phone: 202-331-1619

Offers student loans to U.S. citizens or permanent residents who are in their
final year of their baccalaureate or graduate degree program. Must reside
within the Washington, D.C. metropolitan area. Awards are $5,000 interest-
free loans. Interested students must send a written request (a) giving a brief
personal history; (b) identifying the educational institution attended, subject
studied, date expected to complete studies; and (c) amount of funds needed.

Leopold Schepp Foundation
551 Fifth Avenue, Suite 3000
New York, NY 10176
Phone: (212) 986-3078

Offers scholarships to U.S. citizens enrolled on a full-time basis. Awards are
given to those under 30 pursuing a baccalaureate degree, and those under 40
pursuing a graduate degree. Applicants must demonstrate financial need and
academic excellence. Award amounts are from $500 to $7,500 per student.
Interview is required. Send self-addressed, stamped envelope for application
and information. No firm deadline.

The Paul and Daisy Soros Fellowship for New Americans
400 West 59th Street
New York, NY 10019
Phone: (212) 547-6926
Fax: (212) 548-4623
E-mail: pdsoros_fellows@sorosny.org
www.pdsoros.org

The fellowship consists of a $20,000 maintenance grant and a tuition grant of
one-half of the cost of tuition at the institution the fellow is enrolled in.
Candidates must be holders of green cards, naturalized citizens or children of

two naturalized citizen parents. Students already in graduate study are eligible. You must not be older than 30 years of age.

Agnes Jones Jackson Graduate Fellowship
NAACP
4805 Mt. Hope Drive
Baltimore, MD 21215
Phone: (410) 358-8900
Dr. Beverly P. Cole, Director of Education

Provides $2,000 stipends to members of the NAACP, under 25, who are U.S citizens.

Aspira Association
Grant Vital
1444 I Street, N.W.
Washington, DC 20005
Phone: (202) 835-3600
Fax: (202) 223-1253

Awards are geared toward Puerto Rican and Latino students.

Carl A. Scott Book Scholarship
Council on Social Work Education
1600 Duke Street, Suite 300
Alexandria, VA 22314
Phone: (703) 683-60880
Fax: (703) 683-8099

Available to students from ethnic groups of color (African-American, American Indian, Asian-American, Mexican-American and Puerto Rican) who are in their last year of study for a social work degree in a program accredited by CSWE. Two scholarships in the amounts of $500 each.

Graduate Fellowships Programs
The Wexner Foundation
158 W. Main Street
PO Box 668
New Albany, OH 43054
Phone: (614) 939-6060
www.wexnerfoundation.org
Requires career commitment to Jewish communal service.

HIAS Scholarship Awards
Hebrew Immigrant Aid Society
333 Seventh Avenue
New York, NY 10001-5004
Phone: (212) 967-4100

Visit Vault at **www.vault.com** for insider company profiles, expert advice, career message boards, expert resume reviews, the Vault Job Board and more.

VAULT CAREER LIBRARY   145

Fax: (212) 967-4483
e-mail: info@hias.org

For HIAS-assisted refugees and their children who arrived in the United States. Only those students who immigrated to the U.S. after Jan 1, 2002 are eligible. Send a self-addressed, stamped envelope for information and application. Application can be completed online at hias.org/scholarships/usinfo.html.

National Association of Black Social Workers
Scholarship Committee
8436 West Nichols
Detroit, MI 48221
www.naswbl.org

Students must be African-American and express research interests on African-Americans.

National Association of Puerto Rican Social Workers
P.O. Box 651
Brentwood, NY 11717
Phone: (631) 231-1564
www.naprhsw.com
Att: Pauline Velazquez

Provides scholarship awards to first- or second-year full-time graduate students presently enrolled in a school of social work program. Applicants must be able to demonstrate a strong interest in community organization and community advocacy that would potentially impact the Puerto Rican/Latino community. Applicants should demonstrate financial need and proficient academic performance.

Fellowship on Women and Public Policy
Center for Women in Government
302 Draper Hall
135 Western Avenue
Albany, NY 12222
(518) 442-3383 Fax: 518/422-3877
www.cwig.albany.edu
Dorothy Hogan, Fellowship Program Coordinator

Applicants must have an interest in improving the status of women and underrepresented populations.

National Association of Social Workers — Anne L. Adair Scholarships
This scholarship is offered by the Native Daughters of the Golden West for students enrolled in social welfare education. The applicant must be born in California and other restrictions apply. Call 415.563.9091 for more information.

Women Work
1625 K Street, NW
Washington, DC 20006
Phone: (202) 467-6346
www.womenwork.org

Organization assists women who were homemakers and now need to get a job or go to school to advance in their chosen profession.

An Uncommon Legacy Foundation, Inc.
Scholarship Committee
150 West 26th Street
Suite 602
New York, NY 10001
(212) 366-6507
E-mail: uncmlegacy@aol.com
www.uncommonlegacy.org

Fund for Lesbian and Gay Scholarships (FLAGS)
The Scholarship Fund
PO Box 48320
Los Angeles, CA 90048-0320
(213) 650-5752
Contact: Whitman Brooks

Provides financial assistance to gay, lesbian and bisexual students who are involved in the community.

Alexander Graham Bell Association for the Deaf Scholarship Program
College Scholarship Program
3417 Volta Place, NW
Washington, DC 20002
www.agbell.org

Applicants must be auditory-oral students born with a profound hearing loss or a severe hearing loss and must have experienced such a loss before acquiring language. Scholarships range from $250 to $1,000.

Elmer Edger Memorial Scholarship Fund
Mononite Health Services
PO Box 500
Akron, PA 17501-0550

Candidates must be graduate students who have a vocational interest in mental health, developmental disabilities or related fields, a minimum 3.5 GPA and vital interest and participation in the Christian Church and demonstrate financial need. Scholarships range between $1,000 and $2,000.

Visit Vault at **www.vault.com** for insider company profiles, expert advice, career message boards, expert resume reviews, the Vault Job Board and more.

VAULT CAREER LIBRARY   **147**

National Federation of the Blind Scholarships
805 Fifth Avenue
Grinnell, IA 50112
Phone: (515) 236-3366
www.nfb.org

Awards a broad array of scholarships to recognize achievement by blind
scholars. All applicants for these scholarships must be (a) legally blind and
(b) pursuing or planning to pursue a full-time post-secondary course of study
in the United States, except that one scholarship may be given to a full-time
employee also attending school part time. In addition to these restrictions,
some scholarships have been further restricted by the donor. The scholarship
award is $3,000 to $10,000.

Whitney M. Young Jr. Scholarship Program
National Association of Social Workers
Westchester Division
New York State Chapter
1 Heath Cote Road
Scarsdale, NY 10583
Phone: (914) 725-3610

Provides small stipends to students enrolled in a BSW/MSW program.
Applicants must have a commitment to social work action/change and
maintain standards of excellence, and be recommended by their faculty
advisor.

About the Author

Natalie Wright, LMSW, is a graduate of Columbia University School of Social Work. She works and resides in Brooklyn, NY, where she provides training, staff development and technical assistance at one of the nation's leading providers of victim services.

Visit Vault at **www.vault.com** for insider company profiles, expert advice, career message boards, expert resume reviews, the Vault Job Board and more.

VAULT CAREER LIBRARY 149

Use the Internet's
MOST TARGETED
job search tools.

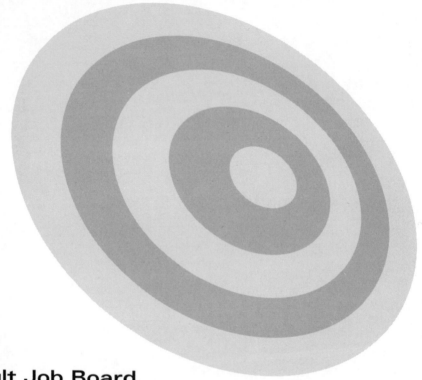

Vault Job Board

Target your search by industry, function, and experience level, and find the job openings that you want.

VaultMatch Resume Database

Vault takes match-making to the next level: post your resume and customize your search by industry, function, experience and more. We'll match job listings with your interests and criteria and e-mail them directly to your inbox.

V/\ULT
> the most trusted name in career information™